In the Founders' Footsteps

LANDMARKS OF THE

AMERICAN REVOLUTION

A. Van Doren

IN
THE FOUNDERS'
FOOTSTEPS

Landmarks of the
American Revolution

ADAM VAN DOREN

with watercolors by the author

Foreword by
NATHANIEL PHILBRICK

Godine · Boston
MMXXII

Published in 2022 by

G O D I N E

Boston, Massachusetts

FRONTISPIECE: Adam Van Doren, *Carpenters' Hall*, 2020

LIBRARY OF CONGRESS CATALOGING-IN-PUBLICATION DATA
Names: Van Doren, Adam, 1962- author, illustrator. | Philbrick, Nathaniel,
writer of preface. | Title: In the founders' footsteps : landmarks of the
American Revolution / Adam Van Doren, with watercolors by the author;
preface by Nathaniel Philbrick. | Description: Boston : Godine, 2022. |
Identifiers: LCCN 2021045630 | ISBN 9781567926620 (hardback)
Subjects: LCSH: Historic sites--United States. | United
States--History--Revolution, 1775-1783--Museums. | United
States--History--Revolution, 1775-1783--Monuments. | United
States--History--Revolution, 1775-1783--Battlefields.
Classification: LCC E289 .V36 2022 | DDC 973.3--dc23/eng/20211027
LC record available at https://lccn.loc.gov/2021045630

First Printing, 2022
Printed in Canada

We come, as Americans, to mark a spot which must forever be dear to us and our posterity. . . . We wish that this structure may proclaim the magnitude and importance of that event to every class and every age.

— DANIEL WEBSTER
from oration given at the commemoration of
the Bunker Hill monument, 1825

CONTENTS

FOREWORD *by* Nathaniel Philbrick   13

INTRODUCTION   17

HISTORIC SITES

THE SWEET PROJECT
Hamilton Grange, *New York City*   33

A LIVING MUSEUM
Colonial Williamsburg, *Williamsburg, Virginia*   39

HALLOWED GROUND
Bunker Hill Monument, *Charlestown, Massachusetts*   43

FATAL MARCH
Benedict Arnold's Trail, *Kennebec River, Maine*
Major Reuben Colburn House, *Pittston, Maine*   49

OF POETS AND GENERALS
Longfellow House–Washington's Headquarters
National Historic Site, *Cambridge, Massachusetts*   55

KNOX'S TRIUMPH
Dorchester Heights Monument, *South Boston, Massachusetts*
Henry Knox Trail, *Great Barrington, Massachusetts*   61

WHERE FREEDOM RANG
Independence Hall, *Philadelphia, Pennsylvania*   67

A NARROW ESCAPE
The Old Stone House, *Brooklyn, New York*   73

THE HIGHER GROUND
Morris-Jumel Mansion, *New York City*   77

FINAL PLEA
  Billop House (Conference House), *Staten Island, New York* 83
TURNING THE TIDE
  Nassau Hall, *Princeton University*
  Clarke House Museum, *Princeton, New Jersey*   91
A TASTE OF HISTORY
  City Tavern, *Philadelphia, Pennsylvania*   97
HOUSE OF WAR
  Cliveden Manor (The Chew House), *Germantown,*
  Pennsylvania   103
WINTER OF DISCONTENT
  Valley Forge Historic Site, *King of Prussia, Pennsylvania* 109
THE GREAT CHAIN
  Hudson River Chain Monument, *West Point, New York*   117
A DARK PAST
  Philipsburg Manor, *Sleepy Hollow, New York*   123
ALLIES IN ARMS
  Rochambeau Monument, *Newport, Rhode Island*   127
WITHOUT MERCY
  Camden Battlefield Site, *Camden, South Carolina*   133
THE SWAMP FOX
  Francis Marion Statue, *Marion, South Carolina*
  City of Charleston, *South Carolina*   137
PLANTER PATRIOT
  George Washington's Gardens, *Mount Vernon, Virginia*   143
A FAMILY LEGACY
  Peacefield (John Adams House), *Quincy, Massachusetts* 149
SOLDIER SPY
  Major John André Monument, *Tappan, New York*
  Yale Art Gallery, *New Haven, Connecticut*   155

MEETING OF MINDS
  Webb Dean Stevens Museum, *Wethersfield, Connecticut*   161
A SECRET SETTING
  Poplar Forest, *Forest, Virginia*   167
THE CROWNING VICTORY
  Yorktown Battlefield Colonial Historical Park,
  Yorktown, Virginia   173
WASHINGTON'S ADIEU
  Fraunces Tavern, *New York City*   179
A MAN FOR ALL SEASONS
  Franklin Court Printing Office, *Philadelphia, Pennsylvania* 185
A NOBLE GESTURE
  Maryland State House, *Annapolis, Maryland*
  Capitol Rotunda, *Washington, D.C.*   191
VOICE OF THE PEOPLE
  Thomas Paine Plaque, *New York City*
  Thomas Paine Monument, *New Rochelle, New York*   195
HERO OF THE SEA
  Crypt of John Paul Jones, United States Naval Academy,
  Annapolis, Maryland
  John Paul Jones Historic House Museum, *Portsmouth,*
  New Hampshire   199

APPENDICES

ADDITIONAL LANDMARKS NOTED IN BRIEF   207
MAPS   214
TIMELINE   217
WHO'S WHO   223
ACKNOWLEDGMENTS   231
SELECT BIBLIOGRAPHY   235

Foreword

NATHANIEL PHILBRICK

I WAS FINISHING my third book about the American Revolution—Washington and Rochambeau were marching toward Yorktown for their climactic confrontation with Cornwallis—when I received a letter from the artist Adam Van Doren. We'd met a few years earlier and I'd since become familiar with his work: paintings of historic buildings that transform wood, stone, iron, and brick into shimmering constructs of color and light. In his most recent book, he'd painted the homes of American presidents; now he wanted to tackle the American Revolution.

Having spent the last decade traveling to battlefields from Pensacola, Florida, to Quebec City, Canada, I immediately started to wonder how Van Doren was going to do it—how was he going to find the visual essence of such a far-flung war? To what sites would he be drawn? Needless to say, I was all in.

IN A LETTER to Thomas Jefferson, John Adams famously claimed that the eight years of war that finally led to America's independence were "no part" of what we call today the American Revolution. The real revolution, Adams maintained, occurred "in the minds of the people . . . before a drop of blood was drawn at Lexington."

But as George Washington, the commander of the army that ultimately brought England to the negotiating table, would have no doubt insisted (had he been alive in August 1815, when Adams wrote to Jefferson, both of them noncombatants), the overthrow of a government cannot be effected merely in a person's mind. For America to win its independence, a war had to be fought—a war that claimed close to seven thousand colonists' lives on the battlefield. Not counted in that number are the estimated seventeen thousand who died as prisoners or from disease. No, the American Revolution was much more than, as Adams maintained, "the steps by which the public opinion was enlightened and informed concerning the authority of Parliament over the colonies." The Revolution required an epic struggle that stretched the length of the eastern United States.

And yet Adams, one of the smartest men ever to have inhabited this land, had a point. Unlike what unfolded in France, where bloody and chaotic social upheaval produced the dictator Napoleon, the American Revolution resulted in a republic, or what Adams called "a government of laws and not of men." For that to happen, however, one extraordinary event had to occur: The leader of the army that had won the War of Independence needed to step aside and hand the reins of government to the appropriate civil official. In this regard, it's possible to view many of the wonderful images in this book as scenes from Washington's almost decade-long journey from Independence Hall in Philadelphia, where in spring 1775 John Adams nominated him to become the leader of the Continental Army, to the Maryland State House, in Annapolis, where on December 23, 1783, Washington surrendered his general's commission to Congress, thereby ensuring that America's embryonic republic would not succumb to a military coup.

It should come as no surprise that one of my favorite paintings in this book is of Washington's Mount Vernon—a house its owner chose to renovate during the Revolution. It's amazing when you think about it: Washington's iconic home acquired its now familiar features—the central pediment in front, a cupola on top, covered arcades connecting the house to the buildings on both sides, and, most distinctive of all, the piazza overlooking the Potomac—amid those turbulent years. This architectural evolution embodies, I believe, what John Adams was getting at when he insisted that the American Revolution was not about a war; it was about what the war created: a government of laws, a house of light beside a wide and gentle river.

Introduction

It is a matter of great good to our souls and of great benefit to our common country . . . that we should, from time to time, gather together and commemorate with reverent minds, and with suitable monuments, those spots which are so blessed as to be particularly identified with the establishment and development of our nation.

—DANIEL BOORSTIN, *The Americans*

WHEN I was thirteen years old, my family went on a vacation during the Bicentennial to Colonial Williamsburg. The restored clapboard houses, unpaved streets, and actors in period costume left a deep impression. But it was a souvenir my father bought me from the gift shop that I remember most. It was a copy of the Declaration of Independence, printed on textured, tea-stained paper meant to look like old parchment (I can still hear the crinkly sound it made). What intrigued me were not the words but the signatures. They were works of art. Benjamin Franklin's had an imaginative flourish, like one of his inventions; John Hancock's had a sweeping "*J*" that exuded real chutzpah ("so fat King George will be able to read it without his spectacles"); John Adams's was quiet and measured, like the humble man he (usually) was. As someone who loved to draw—and was proud of his cursive—I tried to copy them with my pen, pretending perhaps to sport a wig while I did so.

My attempts at forgery did more than improve my handwriting: they opened a window—however tiny and ink stained—into the past. It was a way of making these Founding Fathers human. Without photographs, very little survives that invigorates the solemn images of the Founders we grew up with. Letters, such as in the voluminous correspondence between John and Abigail Adams, give a glimpse into their thoughts. Paintings offer a view of what they looked like, as in Gilbert Stuart's portraits of Jefferson, Jay, Washington, and Monroe, for example.

But historic landmarks—houses, churches, battlefields, taverns, meetinghouses, forts—breathe life into the times of the Founders with a sense of immediacy. Here we can climb the same creaky ladder John Adams did to see a panorama of the new nation from atop Philadelphia's Christ Church; we can stand on the same balcony on which Washington stood at New York City's Morris-Jumel Mansion, as he spied on British maneuvers; we can walk the same winding trail of Paul Revere's midnight ride from Boston; we can sample the same French wines at Monticello that Jefferson brought back from Paris (though perhaps not the same vintage).

Try as it might, YouTube can't replace these sensory experiences. They're the ones that stick. Thus, a few years ago I began a book project on the homes of the American presidents (*The House Tells the Story*, 2016). I spent two years visiting many of these notable residences, among them Mount Vernon, Montpelier (Madison's home), and Peacefield (Adams's home). I documented my discoveries in essays and watercolors. The historian David McCullough, who suggested I write the book, contributed a foreword, and many of the book's pages contain illustrated letters I wrote to him during my travels.

☙

I BECAME INSPIRED. ALTHOUGH I learned much about the American Revolution while I was working on that project, an important question remained. What made these Founders "pledge their lives" for independence? They had much to live for: most of them were wealthy, privileged, and relatively young—their average age was forty-four and Jefferson was only thirty-three. Many of them owned vast estates, which in the case of Montpelier was more than five thousand acres. Some had very large families.

The easy answer is that they believed in something greater than themselves—freedom. But freedom from what? The English were three thousand miles away (a month's travel by ship), and were not exactly ruling excessively heavy-handedly. The colonists on the whole lived well; in fact, the Redcoats who marched through Long Island in August 1776 were surprised to discover that the locals' houses were solidly built and amply furnished, often better than their own. Furthermore, all the colonies enjoyed substantial self-government and the assemblies controlled appropriations that limited the power of the royal governors. Several Founding Fathers—such as Patrick Henry, George Washington, and Thomas Jefferson—were members of the House of Burgesses, the legislative body governing Virginia.

The conflict was that the colonists didn't accept the supremacy of Parliament over their provincial legislatures. Colonists did not have the same rights of representation that English citizens did in Britain. And they didn't always have the right to an immediate trial by a jury. The 1765 Stamp Act is a case in point. It required all printed documents used or created in the colonies to bear an embossed revenue stamp. Stamp Act violations were often tried in vice-admiralty courts because such courts operated without a jury. Colonial assemblies denounced the law, claiming the tax was illegal on the grounds that the American settlers had no representation in Parliament. Many viewed the tax as an infringement of the rights of Englishmen, which contemporary opinion held to be enshrined in the Magna Carta and guaranteed by the Constitution, which had been passed down from the Middle Ages. As a result, protests throughout the colonies threatened tax collectors with violence. In March 1766, Parliament bowed to pressure and repealed the Stamp Act, but the colonial reaction set the stage for the movement for American independence.

In the end, however, freedom is relative. And for many Americans, grievances went beyond taxation without representation. Ultimately, it was about forging a sense of self. Settlers had been arriving since the 1600s, for various reasons and from various countries, to flee religious persecution, to seek land of their own, to escape feudalism; but, for the most part, they had a common bond: that of being *settlers*. They had established a new home in the colonies by clearing forests, building towns, creating farms, trading goods (all at the expense of the Native Americans, who had inhabited these lands for thousands of years), at the same time suffering crippling episodes of famine, sickness, and loss of livestock. Thus, they began to emerge with a new collective identity and a nascent desire to form a new republic. Many of the Founders, therefore, felt a greater connection to their fellow colonists, whose ancestors had toiled to settle the land before them, than to an English king they had never seen. By the middle of the eighteenth century, they considered themselves less and less "Englishmen," at least as it pertained to being British colonists: They considered themselves *Americans*.

Some in Parliament, like Edmund Burke, clearly understood this prevailing sentiment. He voiced opposition to suppressing the Americans' resistance and in January 1775 wrote:

> *I am not here going into the distinctions of rights, nor attempting to mark their boundaries. I do not enter into these metaphysical distinctions; I hate the very sound of them. Leave the Americans*

as they anciently stood, and these distinctions, born of our un-
happy contest, will die along with it. . . . If their freedom cannot
be reconciled . . . they will cast your sovereignty in your face.

But aside from these arguably lofty motives, did the Founders have other, less virtuous reasons to seek independence? Many of them stood to gain personally should the colonists win the war. Without British regulations on trade, the Founders could expand their already-prosperous businesses (one of the signers, Robert Morris, had made a fortune in international shipping). Planters such as Washington operated in constant debt to British agents and suppliers of luxury goods. Like the colonies as a whole, they sold tobacco and raw materials to England at declining prices and paid high sums for British manufactured goods. The war might cancel those debts. In addition, many of the Founders, including Washington, had designs on developing land for profit farther westward unhampered by the Crown's restrictions on expansion, especially the Proclamation Line of 1763 and the Quebec Act of 1774.

Either way, the Founders were taking a bold gamble by starting a revolution. They were pitting themselves against the greatest military in the world, and they barely had an army or a navy. To be sure, the Patriots had fared well at Concord and the Siege of Boston, but those could hardly be considered major battles. Within weeks of signing the Declaration, the English had more than four hundred vessels in New York Harbor, with twenty-four thousand soldiers and ten thousand sailors—more people than made up the entire population of New York City (twenty-five thousand). Furthermore, two thirds of the Americans were ambivalent about the war. As John Adams recalled in a letter to Benjamin Rush years later, "We were about one third Tories [another name for Loyalist], and [one] third timid, and one third true blue." Who, then, would fight? And who would pay for it?

In short, the Americans couldn't pay for it. Their inability to levy taxes limited their coffers. Robert Morris, known as the "Financier of the Revolution," contributed much of his wealth to the cause; and the businessman Haym Salomon, a Jewish immigrant from Poland, added millions (in today's dollars) of his own money. But these men alone were not enough to sustain a war effort that lasted eight long years (and there was speculation that Morris ultimately enriched himself by sending his own cargoes on American vessels at the government's expense). Instead, it would be France, and to a certain extent the Dutch, who offered large loans, that provided the necessary economic support. France's role in the Revolution cannot be overstated. Simply put, without the French, the Americans would have lost. But it would take the victory at Saratoga, in 1777, which proved the colonists could win a major battle, and the diplomacy of Benjamin Franklin, who spent most of the war in Paris, to convince France to join them as an ally.

As the Revolution progressed, the French would also supply soldiers and armaments. The result was a crucial collaboration between George Washington and the French generals Lafayette and Rochambeau. They combined forces to secure victory at Yorktown—a victory that in 1781 would effectively end the war. (Some fighting continued in the Caribbean, however, and it would be another two years before the Treaty of Paris, which would make Great Britain's surrender official.)

For Washington, the Revolution had also been a war of attrition. At times he faced a 20 percent desertion rate, and there was an attempted mutiny of the Pennsylvania regiment at the Morristown winter camp in 1781. Washington's great strength was in keeping the Continental Army together, rallying the troops after the crushing defeat at the Battle of Brooklyn and maintaining morale after two thousand died at Valley Forge.

Often outnumbered and outgunned, Washington somehow persevered, whether it required retreating at White Plains or plotting a surprise attack on Trenton.

This is not to say that Washington didn't occasionally feel hopeless: "In confidence I tell you," he wrote to his cousin Lund Washington on September 30, 1776, "that I never was in such an unhappy, divided state since I was born." Washington never let on to his troops, though. Alexander Milliner, a former soldier in the Continental Army, said in an interview at the age of 104 for an astonishing first-hand account of aged veterans called *The Last Men of the Revolution* (1863): "Washington never changed his countenance, but wore the same in retreat and defeat as in victory."

Washington knew that many of his men would rather be home than on the battlefield. It is optimistic at best to believe that the soldiers of the Continental Army had been racing to enlist, with flags draped over their shoulders. Many of them—newly arrived immigrants, former convicts, or people of poorer means without a trade—were serving simply for the pay, however meager. When their three-year term was up, especially as at Morristown, so was their ambition. Even those who were genuinely inspired by the cause of independence had no stomach for a long war. They had crops to grow and families to feed, and during harvest season, they deserted to attend to both. Some were executed for doing so; others returned to the army with little incident.

Were there exceptions? Ardent Patriots? To be sure. But the reality of a Revolutionary soldier's life is often glamorized. The likelihood of dying—either by disease or in battle—was substantial. A typical battle lasted only a few hours and often engaged only about a thousand men, but the fighting was brutal, often hand-to-hand combat with bayonets. And if you were taken prisoner, you might suffer the fate of wasting away on one of the British ships that had effectively become floating prisons, as more than ten thousand did in New York Harbor and elsewhere.

❧

This volume is an attempt to explore some of the issues mentioned above; it is, in a sense, a sequel to my last book. As with the previous project, it required several visits to historic sites, recording my impressions in situ with words and paints. It would also be an opportunity to meet numerous tour guides, particularly National Park Rangers, who provided invaluable information.

But where to begin?

The list started in my own backyard. I live in New York City. If one were to ask me: "Where did the Revolution happen here?" my answer would be simple. "Everywhere." On East Thirty-fourth Street (the British landing at Kips Bay), where I often see a movie. On the West Side (the Battle of Harlem Heights), where I went to college. At Inwood (the Battle of Kingsbridge), where I've watched football games at Baker Field. In Brooklyn Heights (the Battle of Long Island), where my favorite pizzeria is located. Along the Hudson River (where Cornwallis took Fort Lee), which is only blocks from where I live.

The list goes on. But it's not surprising. The British occupied Lower Manhattan for most of the war, from September 15, 1776, until November 25, 1783, an anniversary celebrated as Evacuation Day until 1914 (in deference to our English allies during the First World War).

Beyond New York, the Revolution raged in many places across America. Boston took center stage, going back to 1770 with the Boston Massacre, the Boston Tea Party, Lexington and Concord, and the Battle of Bunker Hill. But war occurred from Maine to Florida. In South Carolina (Camden, Charleston, Cowpens), according to some historians, more action took place than anywhere else. There were skirmishes as far away as Indiana (Fort Vincennes), Ohio (Fort Laurens), Illinois (Fort Gage), and even Canada (Quebec). To some extent, it was a world war. Admiral John Paul Jones fought the English in the North Sea; the Dutch and Spanish eventually joined the French as American allies; German principalities provided conscripted Hessian soldiers (whose princes profited from their services) to aid the Redcoats.

My list was growing. I decided to divide my landmarks into two groups—the more familiar (Bunker Hill and Valley Forge, for example) and the less well known (such as Cliveden Manor and Carpenters' Hall)—in hopes of appealing to a broad readership. I also chose an iron chain (at West Point); a print shop (Franklin's in Philadelphia); and an oak tree (the Princeton battlefield). I included historic sites from each of the original thirteen colonies and, when possible, ones that referenced African Americans, Native Americans, and women, the foremost of whom was Abigail Adams. At intervals, I noted paintings, literature, and architecture, because history is not just about wars and politics but is also about art. Perhaps of most importance, I selected sites that were accessible to the public.

Armed, then, with my writing notebook and art supplies, I hit the road—sometimes by car, sometimes by train. All told, I traveled more than a thousand miles, and couldn't help but wonder what it was like for Washington on horseback to cover the same distance. He and his men faced muddy farm roads, swollen rivers, and dense forests, sometimes through enemy territory and often at night.

Each place I visited left its mark. At Valley Forge, in Pennsylvania, I toured the log huts and learned how the crowded quarters—twelve men in bunks without windows—fostered the spread of typhoid and typhus. At the Billop House, in Staten Island, I stood in the room where in 1776 General Howe offered an olive branch to three Founding Fathers, who summarily rejected it. At Camden, South Carolina, I discovered how the Patriot fighter Francis Marion used guerrilla tactics to terrorize Colonel Banastre "No Quarter" Tarleton. At Washington's former headquarters in Cambridge, Massachusetts, I was informed about the story of an African American woman who shared her poems with the commander in chief. At City Tavern, in Philadelphia, I met the chef Walter Staib, who prepared period dishes that were favorites of Lafayette. And in Manhattan, a subway ride from my apartment, I toured Alexander Hamilton's house at 143rd Street, which offered a glimpse into the private life of a man who rose from poverty to become America's first secretary of the treasury.

My "walk through history" was illuminating, but it also gave me pause. My sense of the past had changed. I had been taught in school to venerate the Founders as models of virtue through an idealized viewpoint that made me revere my country. But there were great gaps in that history—and much that is disturbing today. The issue of slavery, for one, had been marginalized in my 1970s textbooks. At times, it was framed as a transgression, a forgivable sin that was somehow "of its time." For example, the standard explanation for Washington not freeing his slaves during his or Martha's lifetime was that it was something he couldn't do because slaves under Virginia law were "property." Though it was based in truth, and in fact in his will Washington freed his slaves, the reasoning casually dismissed the amorality of his actions. But as a schoolboy and beyond, I accepted Washington's explanation. Today, I would be less inclined to give him a pass.

Thomas Jefferson, despite being a quintessential Renaissance man, was even worse. In his *Notes on Virginia* (1781), he described African Americans as subhuman, with "inferior" traits. Jefferson also fathered several children with the enslaved Sally Hemings; and he failed to free his 135 slaves (other than Hemings's five children) upon his death.

Native Americans, too, suffered immensely. The Founders participated in a genocidal clearing of their land, often to make way for slave plantations—either by spurious treaties or by force—even after some tribes, such as the Oneida, helped them win the Battle of Saratoga by providing 150 men to General Gates's army. Some scholars regard the Revolution as the Indians' own war of independence: notwithstanding instances like Saratoga, they for the most part sided with the British because they knew the Americans were land hungry and would ultimately displace or destroy them. Even when they gave up their culture and tried to assimilate, they were slaughtered.

And, though they were less persecuted, I wondered about another group: the Loyalists. They were treated as criminals, yet they constituted as much as 30 percent of the population in the colonies. Their grievous offense was an allegiance to the Crown, the only government they'd ever known, whose people spoke their language, wore the same clothes, followed their same system of laws for the most part, and fought on their side during the French and Indian War.

Despite their various failings, however, the Founding Fathers left a legacy of extraordinary achievement. They were some of the most learned men of their age, and they devised a document—the Constitution—that is still the foundation of the United States government. It is a document, furthermore, that stoked the fire of regime change in Japan, Germany, and the Soviet Union during the last century.

As Joseph Ellis, author of *Founding Brothers*, has written in *Britannica*:

> *At the most general level, they [the Founding Fathers] created the first modern nation-state based on . . . the democratic principle that political sovereignty in any government resides in the citizenry rather than in a divinely sanctioned monarchy; the capitalistic principle that economic productivity depends upon the release of individual energies in the marketplace rather than on state-sponsored policies.*

Ellis goes on to list the Founders' other notable successes: they won a war for colonial independence against the most powerful military of the time; they formed the first large republic in the modern world; they created political parties that institutionalized the notion of a legitimate opposition; and they established the concept of the legal separation of church and state. "All these achievements," writes Ellis, "were won without recourse to the guillotine or the firing squad, which is to say without the violent purges that accompanied subsequent revolutions in France, Russia, and China."

Writing this book was not the first time I considered the paradoxes and false narratives of the Founding Fathers as purely heroic figures. Indeed, given the long-overdue national discourse ignited by the Black Lives Matter movement—along with America's history of institutionalized racism and violence toward African Americans—I embraced the opportunity to take an unvarnished look at the Founders. The physical and intellectual tenacity it took to build this republic is certainly nothing short of extraordinary. Yet, when relevant to the context of a particular landmark, it is crucial to our understanding of who we are as a nation to acknowledge the Founders' moral failures. As the documentary filmmaker Ken Burns noted during an interview on CNN in 2020, almost one quarter of our

American presidents were slave owners. "This is a time of reckoning," he said, "and as a white male, I think it's wise to be quiet for the moment and not say anything. I should just try to listen instead."

In the end, however, this book is not intended to overly judge the Founding Fathers. It is meant to gain a deeper understanding of who they were in their time by visiting these historic sites. One such landmark, in retrospect, seems the most poignant. It is one of the least known and is barely noticed by the many people who pass it every day: It's a small plaque to Thomas Paine in New York City at the site of the boardinghouse where in 1809 he died. He was largely forgotten by then, but Paine, whose pamphlets, such as *Common Sense*, reached a vast audience when they were written, had a profound effect on the average American. Wrote the philosopher Sidney Hook in *The Essential Thomas Paine* (1969): "If a man is entitled to be called the Father of American Independence, it is Thomas Paine, whose *Common Sense* stated the case for freedom from England's rule with a logic and passion that roused the public opinion of the Colonies to a white heat."

In the words of Paine himself, from *Common Sense*, 1775–76:

The cause of America is in a great measure the cause of all mankind. Many circumstances have, and will arise, which are not local, but universal . . . The laying of a Country desolate with Fire and Sword, declaring War against the natural rights of all Mankind, and extirpating the Defenders thereof from the Face of the Earth, is the Concern of every Man to whom Nature hath given the Power of feeling.

IN THE FOUNDERS' FOOTSTEPS

Alexander Hamilton found solace in his peaceful abode.

The Sweet Project

HAMILTON GRANGE · *New York City*

I T WAS a perfect late-autumn day in Manhattan, sunny, with bright blue skies, and I'd made plans to visit the home of Alexander Hamilton—also known as "the Grange"— uptown at 148th Street. (The word *grange* once meant "granary," but by Hamilton's time it referred to a barn or farm.) Even though I'd spent four years as a student at Columbia, just a few subway stops from the Grange, I'd never seen it. Considering that Hamilton was Columbia's most famous alumnus and there was a statue of him on campus, it was time to make amends.

I made plans to meet Fred Cookinham, a licensed tour guide who runs In Depth Walking Tours, a company he founded some thirty years ago. I'd been introduced to him by Gary Shapiro, a journalist friend of mine who knows him well. "If you're interested in the colonial period, Cookinham is your man," Gary told me.

I took the subway to meet Fred downtown at Number One Broadway, as he had instructed, and got off at the Bowling Green station. Emerging from the tunnel, I spotted Fred across the street; he was wearing a baseball cap with the name of his company on it. He appeared to be about sixty and had a beard. He was wearing khaki shorts, and with thick-soled boots, he looked ready for a hike on the Appalachian Trail. Over his shoulder was a totebag bulging with three-ring binders. They were filled with maps, photographs, and other archival material.

We shook hands and exchanged a few pleasantries, then Fred got right to work.

The first thing he pointed out was the old Custom House, behind us. It's a handsome Beaux-Arts building, with baroque ornament and large figurative sculptures. "This was designed by Cass Gilbert, who designed the Woolworth Building," Fred told me. "It's now the home of the Museum of the American Indian. In the 1700s, when New York was the capital, the site was set aside for the first White House. But other sites were chosen instead, on Lower Broadway and on Cherry Street— where Washington ultimately lived when he was president. Eventually the capital moved to Philadelphia and then D.C."

Fred pointed out something else. "Look around you," he said. "Much of what you're standing on here is landfill. This isn't where the colonists first lived. They were farther over, near the East River. That area had a better port for sailing ships."

As we headed down a flight of stairs back into the subway and onto a train, I learned more about Fred's background. He was originally from Syracuse and studied history at Cortland State College. He had a master's from Brooklyn College and had written a book on Ayn Rand, another interest of his. He'd been conducting tours continuously since the 1990s, despite his failing eyesight which has kept him from driving.

When we arrived at 154th Street, we began to walk toward the Grange. "Hamilton's house has moved a couple of times," Fred said. "It was first moved in 1889, to a side street next to St. Luke's Episcopal Church at 141st Street, because Manhattan's development was encroaching on it. In 2008, after the house became a National Park site, it was moved again, this time by hydraulic lifts, to St. Nicholas Park, where it is now."

We soon came to a leafy neighborhood of Queen Anne brownstones called, fittingly, Hamilton Heights. As we turned a corner, the Grange came into view. It's set on a low rise, and although the lot is no more than an acre, it's substantial for an urban setting. The entrance gate has a plaque from the National Park Service that reads THE NEW HOME OF THE HAMILTON GRANGE. Rangers were busy installing a planting bed along a newly paved walkway.

The house itself is painted yellow with white trim and has three porches, which were designed to capture views of both the East River and the Hudson. "This was Hamilton's first and only house that he owned," Fred said. "It was his country estate, which he called his Sweet Project, and he spent summers here with his family, taking a carriage from downtown Manhattan, where his office was and where we started today."

As pleasing as the structure is, I noted to Fred, it's not nearly as big as Jefferson's Monticello or Madison's Montpelier.

"Hamilton didn't have the money they did," Fred said. "He was born dirt poor in the West Indies [in 1755 or '57] and was orphaned by the age of thirteen. He was proud to own this property when he did, and went into debt to purchase it. The estate, which he bought in 1799, was once about thirty acres and was planted with thirteen gum trees, symbolizing the thirteen colonies."

This corner of the city, which was once all farmland, is now surrounded by apartment buildings and City College's campus. As we walked around the house, I noticed some peeling paint, and we passed workmen who were shoring it up for restoration.

As we continued to circle the house, Fred pointed out the semi-hexagonal shape of the second-floor bay. "It was the architectural fashion at the time," he said, "to give a house some extra distinction."

The first floor has a gift shop, an exhibition space, and a narrow staircase leading to the second floor. The upstairs has two large brightly painted rooms—one yellow and the other green—with tall French doors that lead to the porches. In another room, every fifteen minutes a movie outlines the particulars of Hamilton's relatively brief life: secretary of the treasury, aide-de-camp to Washington, founder of the National Bank, an author of The Federalist Papers, and founder of a society to free slaves. And that's just scratching the surface.

It seemed fitting that a man of such restless energy would own a house that has been re-located several times. Brilliant, loyal, eloquent, persuasive (though not especially diplomatic), temperamental. These are the characteristics I sensed about him.

Then there was the duel. This is where his sense of honor, another distinctive trait, got the better of him. He was mired in a political dispute with his archrival, Aaron Burr (then vice president), and the two agreed to settle their disagreement with pistols. Dueling was banned in New York, so they met secretly in Weehawken, New Jersey, just across the Hudson. Some say Hamilton missed his shot intentionally; no one will ever know. Burr's bullet struck Hamilton in the abdomen. Rushed back to Lower Manhattan by boat, he was met at the dock by his friend Dr. William Bayard, who insisted that Hamilton be carried to his house on Jane Street in the West Village. He would die there two days later. Last rites were given by Benjamin Moore (son of Clement Moore, who wrote "A Visit from St. Nicholas").

"For years afterward," Fred said, "Bayard's family would show people the bloodstains on the wood floor that had dripped down from the bedroom." Macabre, I thought.

Fred and I headed back to the subway, but he continued to alert me to other points of interest. "At this juncture of St. Nicholas Avenue, the American soldiers marched as prisoners after the Battle of Fort Washington in 1776," he said. "They were forced to camp in a burial ground downtown, the oldest one in the city, which was then a cemetery for Spanish Sephardic Jews who had emigrated in the 1600s."

We got onto the subway car, and as Fred and I sat in our seats, jostling each other on the rumbling No. 1 line, I thought that Hamilton would have been impressed by the speed with which the train crossed the length of Manhattan. During the start of Washington's administration, Hamilton had an office downtown on Wall Street, and it would have taken several hours to travel to the Grange on horseback, a distance of about ten miles. Not an easy commute, especially in those days.

The former colonial capital is now a gallery of restored architecture.

A Living Museum

COLONIAL WILLIAMSBURG · *Williamsburg, Virginia*

COLONIAL WILLIAMSBURG today may seem very quaint and even Disney-like, but during the Revolution it was anything but. Here is where many of the most prominent Founding Fathers, including four future presidents—George Washington, Thomas Jefferson, James Madison, and James Monroe—spoke out against the Crown in the House of Burgesses. Here, in 1774, Virginia's last royal governor, John Murray, Lord Dunmore, dissolved that same legislative body for its solidarity against the Intolerable Acts (punitive measures adopted against the colonists in retaliation for the Boston Tea Party). Here, in 1775, Dunmore, again, dispatched a company of marines to seize the colony's munitions at the public magazine.

Even though the eighteenth-century Williamsburg looks tiny, it was the capital of the colonies from 1699 to 1780 and a significant center of economic and cultural life. One of America's oldest institutions of higher learning, the College of William and Mary, was founded there in 1693, and the first newspaper in America, the *Virginia Gazette*, was published there by William Parkes in 1736. A school, founded by Thomas Bray to educate both free and enslaved Black children, opened its doors in 1760.

With such an importance to history, it's little wonder that

after Williamsburg had fallen into ruin, in the 1800s, great efforts were made to preserve it. The restoration, which transformed the town into a museum, entailed reconstructing scores of buildings—from houses and churches to taverns and shops. And landscaping, too. The gardens and trees that line Duke of Gloucester Street, the main thoroughfare, create, as William Penn promised in the early 1700s for Philadelphia: "a greene country town."

It took decades and well over a billion dollars (in today's money), but when Colonial Williamsburg was completed, in the 1930s, it had two men to thank for its rebirth: William Goodwin and John D. Rockefeller. We all know the Rockefellers as one of the wealthiest families, but who was Goodwin?

He was many things—author, priest, historian—but foremost he was an antiquarian and preservationist. Born in Richmond, Virginia, in 1869, he trained at the Virginia Theological Seminary and while still a teenager developed an interest in colonial history after reading *Buried Cities Recovered* (1882), by Frank De Hass. From 1903 to 1909, he was rector of Williamsburg's Bruton Parish Church (founded in 1674), and would channel that interest into a restoration of the historic building. Before the decade was over, he had conceived a scheme to recreate the entire town of Williamsburg. With the assistance of Rockefeller, whom he enlisted in 1927 to contribute close to $70 million, Goodwin would create a national landmark and become known as the "Father of Colonial Williamsburg."

According to the journalist Walter Karp, in a 1981 article in *American Heritage*:

> For years he [Goodwin] had been in search of a philanthropic Croesus as passionately devoted to restoring old things as Goodwin had been since boyhood. . . . Goodwin wanted his Croesus, as yet undiscovered, to buy up the entire town of Williamsburg and

transform it, lock, stock, and barrel, into the old colonial town
of Williamsburg. He conceived the transformation as a living
monument to the American Revolution.

Rockefeller became his Croesus, although it was not an easy sell. Until then, patriotic causes were not high on Rockefeller's list; he was more interested in saving European monuments. Nevertheless, in 1922, Goodwin persuaded the philanthropist to visit the town. As they walked the streets, Goodwin pointed out the shabby houses, rotted outbuildings, and overgrown gardens—faded remnants of a once-prosperous capital. He spoke of the original town plan, conceived by Governor Francis Nicholson, which after 220 years was still intact.

Rockefeller was convinced. Over time, he bought the existing buildings and gradually donated the full amount necessary to bring the project to fruition.

Colonial Williamsburg today has a prodigious endowment that funds its upkeep and its extensive programming. Scores of actors are employed to dress and act as colonials. They are trained to converse (in character) with visitors and to be, in a sense, teachers. As a visitor twice myself, once with my parents when I was young and again with my own children, I can attest to the lessons learned from these dedicated amateur historians who take their jobs seriously.

During the trip with my children, on the Fourth of July in 2014, we listened as one such actor, Richard Schumann, portraying Patrick Henry (the governor of Virginia in 1776), gave a rousing rendition of Henry's most famous speech. Standing outdoors on a wooden platform, dressed in breeches, wearing a gray cap over a brown wig, and sporting spectacles, he held forth: "Gentlemen may cry, Peace, Peace, but there is no peace! The war is actually begun! . . . Our brethren are already in the field! Why stand we here idle? . . . Forbid it, Almighty God! I know not what course others may take; but as for me, give me liberty or give me death!"

Schumann has been an "interpreter" for a number of years. Speaking with the reporter Deborah Straszheim in a 1998 interview for *The Daily Press*, he described Henry as a "pious man," and though the actor never considered religion much, Schumann said, "now I take it much more seriously." Schumann told Straszheim he found himself living his character—even at home: "It's not at all unusual for my daughters [nine years old at the time] to greet me in the morning with 'Good morrow, Daddy.'"

"The eighteenth century does encroach on your life," added Schumann, who lives fulltime in Williamsburg, "no matter what anyone says."

Williamsburg is that kind of place. It's a cocoon of sorts, where history is the present and time stands still.

Hallowed Ground

BUNKER HILL MONUMENT
Charlestown, Massachusetts

READING ABOUT the Revolution in the cozy confines of an easy chair is one thing. Marching in the heat of battle with muskets firing is another. "The brazen throat of war," as the poet John Milton put it, is a grim business.

The Founding Fathers waxed eloquently about war. But Abigail Adams, the wife of John Adams, got closer to the battlefield than many of them. In a June 18, 1775 letter to her husband, who was in Philadelphia with the Continental Congress, she gives a stirring account of the Battle of Bunker Hill, which she witnessed from her house in Braintree (once part of what is now Quincy), Massachusetts. She writes: "Charlestown is laid in ashes. The Battle began upon our intrenchments upon Bunkers Hill, a Saturday morning about 3 o'clock & has not ceased yet & tis now 3 o'clock Sabbeth afternoon. Tis expected they will come out over the Neck to night, & a dreadful Battle must ensue. . . . How many have fallen we know not—the constant roar of the cannon is so distressing that we can not Eat, Drink or Sleep."

Abigail Adams was actually living with war. The Redcoats had been occupying Boston since 1774. First there was the Boston Massacre, then Lexington and Concord—and then Bunker Hill. In the same June letter to her husband, she pours out her

IN THE FOUNDERS' FOOTSTEPS

feelings: "My bursting Heart must find vent at my pen. I have just heard that our dear Friend Dr. [Joseph] Warren is no more but fell gloriously fighting for his Country—saying better to die honourably in the field than ignominiously hang upon the Gallows. Great is our Loss. He has distinguished himself in every engagement, by his courage and fortitude, by animating the Soldiers and leading them on by his own example."

Abigail was distraught but also stoic. She foresaw, as did so many other Americans at the time, that Bunker Hill was just the beginning of a long, protracted fight for independence. The war would start on April 19, 1775, and end on September 3, 1783. And Bunker Hill was a rallying point early on, one that proved the Patriots' ability to challenge the British on their own terms. By comparison, Lexington and Concord were skirmishes. The outnumbered rebels at Bunker Hill could easily have dropped their arms and fled. No doubt it was menacing to see the glaring red uniforms marching up the hill. But the New Englanders had reached a boiling point and were not deterred.

For the British, Bunker Hill was a rude awakening. Their notion of the Americans as merely "rabble in arms" may have been shattered at Concord, but Bunker Hill would leave the Redcoats stunned. The British general Thomas Gage, commander in chief in North America, had set his sights on gaining the high ground above Charlestown, overlooking Boston, on what is known as Breed's Hill. (Bunker Hill is close to Breed's and a better-known landmark, thus the name stuck.) The rebels, however, got wind of Gage's plan and began to build redoubts to defend the hill. On June 17 the British—cocksure and defiant—brazenly advanced.

The rebels were waiting. William Howe, the British officer who had conceived the plan, acted against all sound military strategy by deciding to march uphill. The Patriots' William

Colonel Prescott stands ready at the base of the memorial obelisk at Bunker Hill.

Prescott is supposed to have ordered: "Don't fire until you see the whites of their eyes, and then aim low" (some historians attribute this quote to Israel Putnam, who was a general in the American army). As the Redcoats came closer, the Americans fired down at them at will. The field that was supposed to be the passage for a flanking attack by the regulars became a stage for slaughter. It would require three attempts before the British won the hill: the Americans, finally out of ammunition, had to retreat.

On paper, the Redcoats had won, but the Battle of Bunker Hill would be considered an American victory. The number of casualties inflicted by the provincial solders from Massachusetts, Connecticut, and New Hampshire were staggering. Of the some twenty-four hundred British soldiers and marines engaged, more than a thousand were wounded or killed. One British officer was moved to quote Falstaff: "They make us here but food for gunpowder."

Fifty years after the the bloody fight, the Marquis de Lafayette, the French general who had joined the American cause in 1775 and become Washington's close confidant, set the cornerstone of what would be a lasting monument and tribute to the memory of the historic battle. The project was ambitious: a 221-foot-tall obelisk built entirely from quarried granite. It took more than seventeen years to complete, and it stands to this day atop the battlefield.

Several years ago, I took my children to see the site. It was a sunny day, and the obelisk, looming over a statue of Prescott, was bright white against the blue sky. My son Henry, who was ten, challenged me to climb with him the 294 steps to the top, and I accepted.

When I got to the summit (Henry was already there), I immediately looked for a spot to sit down. As I caught my breath,

I thought about the long walk up. The effort was draining, but hardly comparable to what the soldiers must have endured during battle. That realization, however, would have to be pondered back in the comforts of my chair.

But let me give Abigail the last word. In a letter to John, she quotes a poem by William Collins (1721–1759), a noted poet in her day:

> *How sleep the Brave, who sink to rest*
> *By all their Country's wishes blest?*
> *When Spring, with dewy fingers cold,*
> *Returns to deck their Hallowed mould,*
> *She there shall dress a sweeter Sod*
> *Than Fancy's feet have ever trod.*

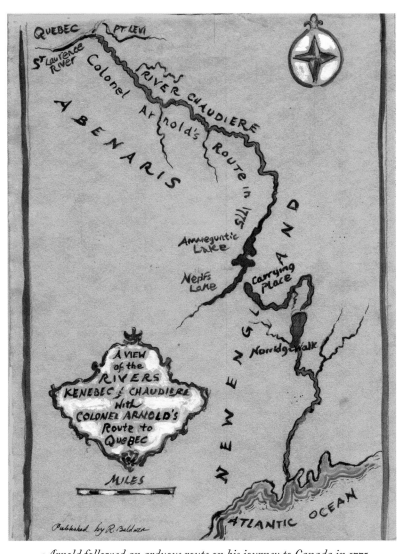

Arnold followed an arduous route on his journey to Canada in 1775.

Fatal March

BENEDICT ARNOLD'S TRAIL · *Kennebec River, Maine*
MAJOR REUBEN COLBURN HOUSE · *Pittston, Maine*

ONE OF the most harrowing military expeditions of
the Revolution was the Americans' march to Quebec
in fall 1775. It was an early attempt to attack the British at their fortifications in Canada, and though an ill-fated
campaign, it was significant in the struggle for independence.
The long trek, which began in Massachusetts, was supposed
to take three weeks but lasted six. Of the eleven hundred men
who journeyed the 350 miles through thick woods and deep
ravines, only half made it. Starvation forced them to eat shoe
leather, shaving soap, candle wax, even their dogs. In addition,
many of their bateaux, or flatboats, sank in Maine's Kennebec
River, losing vital provisions.

The fact that anyone survived is a miracle, and a testament
to the men's commanding officer, Benedict Arnold.

To many Americans, it's difficult to imagine Arnold as a
hero—his very name is synonymous with the word *traitor*—
but at one time he was admired by none other than George
Washington. Washington considered him among his finest
officers, even a friend. Arnold's surprise attack on May 10,
1775, on Fort Ticonderoga with Ethan Allen and the Green
Mountain Boys was crucial to supplying the Continental
Army with much-needed artillery. Arnold was savvy, intelli-

gent, ambitious, even charming. He and Washington enjoyed a mutual respect: "They were brothers in arms, as strange as that sounds," the historian Jim Martin told me over the phone in 2020. "The two of them got to know each other when they first met at Washington's headquarters in Cambridge, during the Siege of Boston [April 19, 1775–March 17, 1776], and together they became very effective."

Jim Martin is a professor history at the University of Houston. He's the author of *Benedict Arnold: An American Warrior Reconsidered* (1997) and eleven other books, among them *A Respectable Army: The Military Origins of the Republic, 1763–1789* and *Forgotten Allies: The Oneida Indians and the American Revolution.*

"Arnold was actually involved in the Revolutionary War before Washington," he told me. "Remember: Washington doesn't become commander of the Continental Army until June of 1775; Arnold had already been in the North before then and captured Ticonderoga. . . .

"Arnold was outspoken that the Redcoats must be forced out of Canada," Jim continued. "He foresaw that if the British controlled the northern rivers, they could access New York and split the colonies in two. He knew that it was essential to attack Quebec City, which England had occupied since its victory in the French and Indian War."

Arnold also knew that such an expedition required money and men. Each was scarce, but Washington made sure he got both. Money, in particular, was a challenge, because Congress did not have the power to tax the colonists and thus relied on a small war chest. Congress was forced to print more currency than it had, which resulted in hyperinflation. Congress did, however, muster what it could to provide for Arnold's expedition, for it had long plotted for Canada to join America as the fourteenth colony. On November 19, 1775, Thomas Jefferson would write: "In a short time, we have reason to hope, the delegates of Canada will join us in Congress and complete the American union as far as we wish to have it completed."

Arnold's expedition to Quebec left from Cambridge, Massachusetts, on September 15, 1775, with little fanfare. Many of the men armed themselves with rifles, tomahawks, and scalping knives, like the local Native Americans. Within three days, they arrived at Newburyport, at the northeastern corner of the state. From there, the party sailed twelve hours along the upper New England coast, then headed inward to the mouth of the Kennebec River, which cuts north through what is now west-central Maine.

It was there that their troubles began. Not long after sailing along the shoals, the soldiers found themselves in dense, harsh wilderness, wading through frigid water and rapid currents. Some of their bateaux were immediately crushed. Steadily, the mission grew worse. The old Indian trails through the woods were washed out by driving rains. When they finally reached Quebec, many of the men were too exhausted to move. One first-person account of these hardships was recorded in the diary of Abner Stocking, a twenty-two-year-old soldier from Chatham, Connecticut:

On November 2 he wrote, "When we arose this morning many of the company were so weak that they could hardly stand on their legs. When we attempted to march, they reeled about like drunken men, having now been without provisions for five days. As I proceeded I passed many sitting, wholly drowned in sorrow."

And on November 8: "Our clothes were torn to pieces by the bushes, and hung in strings—few of has had any shoes, but moggasons made of raw skins—many of us without hats—and beards long and visages thin and meager. I thought we much resembled the animals that inhabit New-Spain, called Ourang-Outang."

Other period diaries chronicle the plight of these men. Each is an important historical document. But if we fast-forward to modern times, we discover a fresh account of this march that is also of interest. It comes, again, from Professor Martin. He has followed the trail not once but three times. "I'm a lifetime member of the Arnold Expeditionary Society," Jim told me. "I first took the trail with my daughters in the 1990s, and then I did it again with a tour group in 2001. I returned a few years later on my own. Granted it was mostly by car, but you still get a good sense of how difficult the march was, especially without any passable roads."

I asked Jim if there were some noteworthy sites he could recommend. "Many of the locations where Arnold went on his journey are still there," he said, "especially the dramatic natural scenery along the Kennebec River. You can see how the fierce current of the whitewater was a trial for Arnold and his men, especially because their boats were hastily assembled and made with green wood. The Great Carrying Place, so called, and the Dead River are sites worth exploring. Along the way there's the place called Colburn House, where Arnold stayed when he built the bateaux. It's one of the oldest houses in Maine and now a museum. You can also visit Fort Western, another stop on their trail, which has been restored. These landmarks all look quaint now, but they were once part of a real nightmare."

It's not surprising that Jim sees the inherent drama in Arnold's expedition. He has written several screenplays on historical topics and knows a good plot when he sees one. He also knows a thing or two about acting—and Arnold's is surely a leading role.

"Washington considered Arnold his greatest fighting general," Jim told me. "He was a hard driver and very skilled. And relentless. He was also hotheaded and made enemies easily. He believed in a gentleman's honor and engaged in a number of duels."

"Why do you think he became a turncoat?" I asked.

"It's complicated," he replied, "but I think he felt slighted and underappreciated for his role at the battle of Saratoga. General Gates got most of the credit, but Arnold felt he deserved the laurels because he fought much more in the field. Arnold came from a well-to-do Connecticut family and thought highly of himself. But he was restless. Even when he was promoted, he was unhappy. He was enormously ambitious and tough but also thin-skinned."

As for the outcome of Arnold's march, the story ends badly. When the army finally reached Quebec City, it was forced in late December to fight during a blinding blizzard. The soldiers attempted strikes on Lower Town and then the fort on the hill, but the British, under Guy Carlton, resisted and eventually prevailed. Arnold was severely wounded and his fellow commander Richard Montgomery, who had brought reinforcements from Montreal, was killed. Retreat was the only recourse.

"Was the expedition, then, worth the effort?" I asked.

"Well, it was a failure in many respects," said the professor, "but the Americans did buy some time for the Siege of Boston, and it managed to keep the British from advancing from the north any farther. At the same time, the expedition took its toll, and Washington lost many men whom he needed."

A bust of Washington welcomes visitors to the old manse in Cambridge.

Of Poets and Generals

LONGFELLOW HOUSE–WASHINGTON'S
HEADQUARTERS NATIONAL HISTORIC SITE
Cambridge, Massachusetts

Through the open doors
The harmless phantoms on their errands glide,
With feet that make no sound upon the floors . . .

THESE LINES are from "Haunted Houses," written by
Henry Wadsworth Longfellow in 1857. At the time, he
was living in Cambridge, Massachusetts, in a house he
had already owned for more than twenty years. If you know the
history of the dwelling, as I do, you might imagine that the author had certain people in mind when he composed those lines.
We'll never know for sure, but I like to think that one of the
"harmless phantoms" was George Washington. Washington,
after all, lived in that very house for over eight months from
July 1775 to April 1776, when it was his headquarters during the
Siege of Boston, when the British were blockading what we
now call the downtown.

Longfellow was a proud steward of the Washington legacy.
For many years he kept a bust of the general at his stair landing
and hung various prints of him in the front hall. He relished
the fact that his maternal grandfather, Peleg Wadsworth, was
an officer in Washington's Continental Army.

The Longfellows kept the house in the family until 1913,

when they created a trust to preserve it. It was sold, in 1972, to the United States government as a national landmark. Today it is called the Longfellow House–Washington's Headquarters National Historic Site. It's on Brattle Street, near Harvard Square, and as a child growing up in Cambridge in the 1960s, I remember walking by it often. I was too young to appreciate its significance, but I could tell even then what an impressive home it was, with its lemon yellow siding, large white windows, and tall chimneys. It was set far back from the curb, just down the street from the Design Research furniture store, a Brutalist-style building that provided a stark contrast to the Georgian Colonial.

Preservationists over the last several decades have worked diligently to keep the residence open to the public. The late senator Ted Kennedy, a noted proponent of history education, was among the more outspoken who stressed the need to support this prime national treasure.

The house had ties to the Revolution even before Washington occupied it. It was built in 1759 for John Vassall, a Loyalist who fled across the Charles River to Boston for safety. After he died, in 1772, in England, his property was confiscated and in 1774 was sold at auction. The home was later used as a temporary hospital after the clashes at Lexington and Concord. In June 1775, Brigiadier General John Glover and his Massachusetts regiment occupied the house as their temporary barracks.

A month before Washington moved in (after staying at the Wadsworth house at Harvard, which was too small), he had been named commander in chief of the Continental Army. (John Hancock had been considered for the post, but he lacked military experience). The Revolution was in its early stages, but already some key battles had taken place, such as the Battle of Bunker Hill (June 17, 1775). For much of the remaining year and into the next, Washington plotted strategy, kept up his correspondence with Congress, and worked on organizing his army. His men were a motley crew, and the courtly Virginian had little patience for the uncouth New Englanders. Writing to his cousin Lund Washington on August 20, 1775, General Washington described them as "a numerous army of Provincials under very little command, discipline, or order." Occasionally he questioned why he had undertaken such a grave responsibility. In that same letter he added: "I have often thought how much happier I should have been if I could return to the back country and live in a wigwam."

But when the future president was not burdened by his lackluster army or the demands of his position, he found time to enjoy himself, especially when his wife was present. Martha Washington journeyed that December 1775 from Mount Vernon to spend a few months with him. Despite the difficulty of traveling by horse and carriage over unpaved, often muddy roads, she did not come empty-handed. Containers of food and other stores accompanied her, boosting the morale of Washington's officers and soldiers alike.

General and Mrs. Washington were frequent hosts for sumptuous dinner parties and dances, with friends such as John and Abigail Adams, Brigadier General Henry Knox, and Major General Nathanael Greene. Records show an order of food supplies that included lamb, roasted pigs, wild ducks, geese, turtles, cider plums, and "a load of liquor from Beverly [Massachusetts]."

But of all the people Washington invited to his quarters, perhaps the most remarkable was an African American poet named Phillis Wheatley. In October 1775, she wrote a letter to the general and enclosed a poem she had composed about him. "Wishing your Excellency all possible success," she began, "in the great cause you are so generously engaged in." The final stanza from her poem read:

Proceed, great chief, with virtue on thy side,
Thy ev'ry action let the Goddess guide
A crown, a mansion, and a throne that shine,
With gold unfading, WASHINGTON! Be thine!

Washington was sufficiently impressed that he replied to her, in February 1776. "I thank you most sincerely for your polite notice of me," he wrote, "in the elegant Lines you enclosed . . . the style and manner exhibit a striking proof of your great poetical Talent. . . . If you should ever come to Cambridge, or near Head Quarters, I shall be happy to see a person so favoured by the Muses."

Born in Senegal about 1753, Wheatley is considered the first African American to publish a book of poems. She was kidnapped as a small child in 1761 and taken to Boston on a slave ship. There she was purchased by John Wheatley, in whose home she was educated in Latin and Greek. Her first and only volume, *Poems on Various Subjects, Religious and Moral,* was printed in 1773, when she was barely twenty. It soon established her reputation. The writer Alice Walker wrote in *In Search of Our Mothers' Gardens* (1983) that "had she [Wheatley] been white, she would have been easily considered the intellectual superior . . . of most of the men of the society of her day."

There is no record that Wheatley actually visited Washington's headquarters, but it is noteworthy that the general, who owned more than three hundred slaves, had such respect for Wheatley's intellect. Was it out of vanity that he admired her work? I think it was genuine, but it reminds us that Washington—an American we've been taught to revere as a Founder—was also part of a cruel and indefensible system of racism and economic opportunism whose grave consequences are still playing out.

Washington would vacate the house on Brattle Street shortly after securing the high ground at Dorchester Heights, in March 1776, and driving the British from Boston.

It would make for an important stage in the War of Independence, but it was only the beginning.

Oxen haul a dismantled cannon from Fort Ticonderoga over mountains and snow (after a painting by Tom Lovell).

Knox's Triumph

DORCHESTER HEIGHTS MONUMENT
South Boston, Massachusetts
HENRY KNOX TRAIL · *Great Barrington, Massachusetts*

THERE'S AN old road through western Massachu-setts that's barely findable today. It's a patchwork of highways, housing lots, overgrown brush, and shop-ping malls. But it once witnessed one of the great stories of the American Revolution.

Over six weeks during the winter of 1775, the Patriot gen-eral Henry Knox and his soldiers used this byway to transport twenty-six cannons on a secret mission from Fort Ticonderoga to Boston, a distance of three hundred miles. These cannons, abandoned after the French and Indian War, were needed for an attack against the British who occupied Boston. The Con-tinental Army was in short supply of such artillery because America had few means to manufacture heavy guns. There were only a few iron furnaces in the colonies, mostly in Connecticut and along the Hudson River.

Knox and his men used oxen and wooden sleds to carry the cannons, dismantled for easier conveyance, across snow and ice. They often traveled at night, to avoid the enemy, with only lan-terns to guide them. Today, with trucks and trains, it would take less than a day. But considering the available transporta-tion of the 1700s, Knox's achievement was epic. And all the more so because Knox, a former bookseller in Boston, had only an informal military training: he was self-taught from all those books in his shop.

Knox devised the scheme with Washington's approval. During that time, the middle of 1775, more than a hundred British warships were anchored at Boston—a daunting show of force—but the Patriots remained steadfast. Washington, however, could wait only so long. He was weary of the stalemate, and many of his men's term of service was about to end. Who would blink first? Washington had barely any navy. But he was at his best when he had the least to work with.

He liked his chances if he could gain higher ground. Dorchester Heights, just south of Boston, was it. There he could install cannons to fire down on the city. The British frigates in the bay were also targets. He hoped the ships would attempt to attack the heights, in which case Washington could easily destroy them.

Tom Wicker writes in an essay in *Forgotten Heroes* (1998), "The sheer size and weight of this cargo and the arduousness of the impending journey, even for an unburdened party on horseback, would have intimidated most men. But one of the characteristics that attracted Washington to Knox was his ebullient optimism."

When the almost sixty tons of artillery finally reached their destination—at a site near Roxbury, just outside of Boston—the guns were kept hidden for several weeks before being deployed. When the day in March arrived to move them, Washington had to be cautious. The British must not discover what he was plotting. His men wrapped straw around the wagon wheels of the now-assembled cannons to deaden the sound as they rolled.

Abigail Adams, whose letters to her husband chronicled the home front during the Revolution, wrote of the arrival of Knox and his cannons, "I look forward to it with a mix of trepidation and excitement."

The British woke up the following day and were caught unawares. As Washington wrote to John Hancock, president of the Congress, on March 7, 1776: "When the enemy first discovered our Works in the morning they seemed to be in great confusion." To make matters worse for the British, a violent storm came up, preventing them from landing and attacking Dorchester Heights for a preemptive strike. The English evacuated Boston, and this was an early turning point in the war for the Americans, who had now outmaneuvered the most powerful army on earth.

Bernard Drew, a historian and the author of *Henry Knox* (2012), is a resident of Great Barrington, Massachusetts, near where Knox passed through with his men during their arduous trek. Bernard has spent years studying the details of the journey. I reached him by phone in the late autumn of 2019.

"I called it the war road," he told me. "It goes back to the French and Indian War and to the Puritans before that. Originally, I was going to write about the entire route Knox took through Massachusetts, but it was too much to tackle. I had enough to cover with the stretch of eighteen miles I worked with."

The historian, who has written or edited ten other books, including *Literary Luminaries of the Berkshires* (2015), spoke of alternative trails Knox could have taken, such as the Mohawk Trail. "It was much steeper, though," he said, "and would've been harder to cross, especially in winter. Knox wanted to move as quickly as possible, because he was afraid of Loyalists along the way who might ambush him and his men. To be sure the country was divided among those who supported the Crown, those who were rebels, and those who were on the fence. But Knox had nothing to fear; it was mostly Patriots along the route."

I asked him if he gained a greater appreciation for what Knox did by following the trail.

"Yes, definitely," he said. "Knox faced incredible obstacles. He wrote in a letter to his wife that he 'almost died from the cold.' And at one point an eighteen-pounder [a type of cannon that was often used on naval ships] fell through the ice while crossing the Mohawk River." But, he added, "I also gained an appreciation for the ones before Knox, who had traveled this road and made it passable."

"Is there any physical evidence left of the trail?" I asked.

"Yes, at several points along the road there are historical markers made out of granite," he said. "Some of them have bronze-relief carvings. They're worth seeing."

He talked more about the history that remains. "Overall, though, it's a sparse record," he said. "Very little survives of Knox's journals or letters, so it was a challenge to put the pieces together. If you want to get a better sense, you can visit his house in Maine, which was rebuilt after being demolished in 1929."

I set out to learn more about the house. My research uncovered that Knox retired in 1795 to a large tract of land in what is now Thomaston, Maine. His wife had inherited the property from her mother, and Knox built on it an elaborate, nineteen-room mansion and named it Montpelier. He became active in local affairs and was involved in the area's development. He shipped timber, made bricks, built a lock-and-canal system on the Georges River, and quarried lime. He helped found a church, too.

Knox died at the age of fifty-six. A fine portrait by Gilbert Stuart hanging at the Boston Museum of Fine Arts shows him in full regalia as one of the Revolution's greatest heroes. After the War of Independence, Knox served as secretary of war under Washington. He participated in the ratification of the Massachusetts Constitution and in 1786 would play a significant role in suppressing Shays' Rebellion, an armed uprising in western Massachusetts stemming from a debt crisis among farmers.

But if Knox had done nothing else in his life but transport those cannons from Ticonderoga, his fame would be secure. Certainly that was the opinion of George Washington, who wrote in a letter to John Adams many years later on September 25, 1798: "There is no one who I have loved more sincerely."

The Declaration was signed in this historic landmark.

Where Freedom Rang

INDEPENDENCE HALL · *Philadelphia, Pennsylvania*

WHEN I was young, in the 1970s, during the summer my parents and I often went to New York from our home in Evanston, Illinois. We stayed in Midtown, where my grandmother had a spacious apartment overlooking West 57th Street. Our usual stomping grounds were the Russian Tea Room, Carnegie Hall, Lee's Art Shop, and the Colosseum Bookstore. A highlight was taking in a Broadway show. One that sticks in my mind was *1776*.

The production, written by Peter Stone with music and lyrics by Sherman Edwards, was about the signing of the Declaration of Independence. It opened in 1969 at the 46th Street Theater (now the Richard Rogers Theater) and ran for 1,271 performances. I still have the *Playbill*, with an illustration of a bald eagle chick holding an American flag in its beak. William Daniels played John Adams, Howard Da Silva played Franklin, and Ken Howard played Jefferson. I remember well the opening number, "Sit Down, John," which featured Adams's contentious character (portrayed as a zealous advocate of independence) and it became the production's best-known song.

I remember the stage set, too. It was the main chamber of Independence Hall, with its high ceiling, tall windows, and gilded chandeliers. The principal actors each played a member of the Continental Congress. They had their own desk, a Windsor chair, and a candlestick—and of course a quill pen. Some held a small fan to ward off the oppressive heat during the days leading to July 4. For many years afterward, whenever I read books about the Declaration, I envisioned that set and thought of the lyrics:

> *For God's sake, John, sit down!*
> *Someone oughta open up the window!*
> *It's ninety degrees!*
> *Have mercy, John, please*
> *It's hot as hell in Philadelphia!*

It would take me fifty more hot summers, but in June 2019 I finally got to see Independence Hall. My friend Bob Demento, a native Philadelphian, had generously arranged a private visit for me. Bob has a particular interest in the Revolution and knows many of its notable sites. He's an active member of the Library Company, the oldest library in America (founded by Franklin), and the Thomas Jefferson Foundation. Bob had contacted Cynthia MacLeod, a National Park Ranger, to conduct the tour.

On a bright morning Bob and I met Cynthia at the entrance to the large Georgian structure in what is known as Independence National Historic Park. She was wearing an olive green uniform and a beige Stetson hat. She greeted us with a warm southern accent and we soon got to talking about how she became a ranger. "I'm originally from Charlottesville," she said. "I got my master's in decorative arts, and my husband is an architect in the city specializing in preservation, so I've spent a lot of time in landmark buildings."

As a throng of tourists starting filing in, Cynthia led us to the head of the line to avoid the crowds. It was nice to get the VIP treatment. When we passed through the front hall, we came to the main room (now roped off), where the Declaration was signed. It was moving to see where the Founding Fathers spent more than a month discussing, arguing about, and finalizing the historic document. Richard Henry Lee, delegate from Virginia, made the motion for independence in early June that triggered the debate. Shortly thereafter, Jefferson began work on his first draft.

I stepped back to admire the architecture, with its raised-panel walls, wide-wood flooring, and grand fireplace. The space was much bigger than I'd imagined. I noticed a large chair on a platform. "That's where Washington sat when he presided over the Constitutional Convention," Cynthia told us. "He was not present for the Declaration, because he was off fighting the war."

"Yes, of course," I said, not admitting I hadn't thought of that.

"Ben Franklin often fixed his stare at the chair during the Convention," said our guide. "He wasn't sure if the decorative image on it was 'of the rising sun—or the setting sun.' After the Convention was over, he declared: 'Now I know: it's the *rising* sun.'"

Cynthia explained that the other pieces of furniture were replicas. I was disappointed; I'd have preferred the real ones, rickety and worn with age. But this didn't squelch my desire to sit at one of the wood tables and imagine what is was like to be a Founding Founder, though of course the guard wouldn't have allowed me to finagle a seat. In any case, I was startled to see how close together the chairs and tables were. Given the tension and heat of July 1776, it's a wonder the proceedings didn't turn to fisticuffs.

Cynthia then took Bob and me up a grand staircase at the opposite end of the hall. A large Palladian window with white trim filtered a gauzy light onto the landing. We walked up to the second floor to a spacious room with a long table.

"This is where the Daughters of the American Revolution meet every year," she said. "You have to have a lineal descendant from the Patriots of the Revolution to be a member. The group's annual meeting is coming up soon."

We then entered the room where the House of Representatives met after the Revolution. Another Park Ranger was already leading a tour, of some middle school children. When the ranger quizzed the kids about what the Thirteenth Amendment to the Constitution did, one young boy answered quickly and correctly: It abolished slavery.

When we returned to the front of the building, Cynthia mentioned that every year on July 4 a special presentation takes place there: A descendant of Colonel John Nixon, an officer in the Revolution, gives a public reading of the Declaration. "The last time it was Jay Nixon, who's the governor of Missouri. It's a nice tradition, and I hope they keep it going," she said.

Our final stop was next door, where an original copy of the Declaration is on display in a wing of Independence Hall. It's set in a dimly lit exhibition case, to protect the ink from fading, with bulletproof glass. A couple of guards keep a close watch. It reminded me of seeing the Crown Jewels in the Tower of London. We joined the line.

When it was my turn, I stepped up to the case and peered at the document, one of only thirteen signed copies (one for each of the colonies). It was thrilling to get that close to the original. There, in front of me, were the unmistakable signatures of Hancock, Franklin, and Adams. I took a moment to read the opening words, in their florid script: "When in the course of human events…" They held a deeper meaning to me on the handwritten page, as had the Gettysburg Address when I saw it in an exhibition at the Smithsonian in 2009. The internet is fine if you can't get to see these documents in person, but for a sense of living history, there's nothing like the real thing.

Cynthia then excused herself; she had an appointment with another tour group. Bob and I thanked her and headed back out to the street—and the noonday sun. "How about sitting down to grab a bite and cool off?" said Bob. "I know a great place that's not far. It's been around forever. It's called Franklin's Ice Cream." Of course.

The rebels fight valiantly in a losing cause at Brooklyn
(after a painting by Dominick D'Andrea).

A Narrow Escape

THE OLD STONE HOUSE · *Brooklyn, New York*

Y OU CAN'T underestimate the role that luck plays in history, especially when you think of George Washington at the Battle of Brooklyn. If it weren't for an early-morning fog, the American Revolution might have ended then and there.

The battle, also called the Battle of Long Island, was the first major one the Continentals fought after the signing of the Declaration. It remains one of the lesser-known of the War of Independence, and yet it was one of the largest and arguably the most important. Some thirty thousand men were engaged—twenty thousand British and Hessians and almost ten thousand Americans. The outcome was a resounding British victory. But there was that fog . . .

At the end of the battle, which took place August 27, 1776, Washington found himself with a thousand dead, wounded, or captured. He was backed up against the East River, with General William Howe closing in. Lesser generals might have surrendered, but America's first president-to-be had planned an exit strategy. Aided by Brigadier General John Glover and his regiment of mariners from Marblehead, Massachusetts, Washington rounded up boats of all kinds from the townspeople and anyone else who owned one. Throughout the night, Washington's men were ferried across the choppy waters. At first light, the boats were still transporting men. Washington left a thousand soldiers in Brooklyn to build fires and make noise to mask the retreat. If the British caught sight of the evacuation, the last thousand would be lost.

Then—at the perfect moment—a morning fog rolled in, obscuring the troops' movements. All but a couple of men reached safe harbor. Washington remained on the Brooklyn side until the mission was complete. It was the Dunkirk of the American Revolution. When the Redcoats awoke the next day, they found that the Americans had disappeared. They were stunned. How could they have let them slip away?

There was plenty of blame to go around, but the English, in their defense, suffered significant casualties themselves (more than four hundred men), and they were still nursing their wounds. Furthermore, their plan had never been to annihilate the rebels; they were, after all, still British subjects.

Nevertheless, historians have questioned why the British didn't crush their adversaries when they had the chance. Howe, it seems, had grossly underestimated America's generals, particularly one Lord Stirling. Stirling is not a household name today, but his fifteen minutes of fame undoubtedly took place during the Battle of Brooklyn. If his lofty title seems odd for an American, there was a reason for it. Stirling, who was born in New York City, in 1726, called himself Lord because he believed he descended from Scottish nobles. Whether or not he deserved such a title, he distinguished himself in a manner becoming of nobility. He valiantly led the Maryland regiment at Brooklyn with repeated attacks on a British position, near what is known as the Old Stone House, a seventeenth-century Dutch farmstead. At one point, his four hundred men were pitted against two thousand of the British. The Marylanders fell, regrouped, and attacked again, but their losses proved too great and Stirling was forced to surrender. Said General Cornwallis: "Stirling fought like a wolf."

Stirling's men have been called "the Maryland 400," after the Spartan stand against the Persians at the Battle of Thermopylae, when three hundred of these ancient warriors fought to the death against overwhelming odds. According to some accounts, more than 250 of Stirling's men died. Their resting place has never been found. The last official archaeological excavations, conducted in the 1950s, failed to turn up any evidence of military burials.

The Old Stone House is a reconstruction that marks the place in Washington Park, on the border of Park Slope and Gowanus, where the original stood. The first owner of the house, Hendrick Claessen Van Vechten, was a wealthy citizen of what was then known as Breukelen. His son Nicholas lived in the house with his wife, Abigail, throughout the Revolutionary War.

The building is now listed on the National Register of Historic Places. But for those who have further interest in the actual battle, there is a curious and somewhat eccentric film called *The Brave Man*, made in 2001 by Joe McCarthy. The thirty-minute movie is unusual in that it incorporates period costumes and yet was filmed in modern-day Brooklyn. In one scene, Stirling, played by the actor Graeme Malcolm, marches through traffic along a main street, flanked not by open fields but by delis and taxis. McCarthy, in an interview on *Fresh Air* for NPR in August 2001, noted that as remarkable as it might seem, you can still sense (albeit with some little imagination) the topography of Brooklyn where the fighting took place. The director also said it was considerably cheaper to set the film in the present, as opposed to building historically accurate sets.

Washington's bedroom at Morris–Jumel povided a quiet respite during the New York campaign.

The Higher Ground

MORRIS-JUMEL MANSION · *New York City*

G EORGE WASHINGTON covered a lot of ground during his lifetime, even for someone on horseback. In his days as a surveyor, planter, soldier, and statesman, he traveled extraordinary distances, from the backcountry of Virginia and Pennsylvania, to the coasts of Rhode Island and Massachusetts. It's no wonder that "Washington Slept Here" has become part of our lexicon.

This Founding Father, however, unknown to many, slept many of his nights in New York City. For almost two years, during his term as president (1789–97), he lived in a mansion on Cherry Street, the first "White House" in the United States (the District of Columbia was not yet the nation's capital). He worshipped at St. Paul's Chapel on lower Broadway and attended a commencement of Columbia College (formerly King's College) in 1789. He had the Declaration of Independence read to his army in front of what is now City Hall Park. He fought in the Battles of Harlem Heights, Kips Bay, and Brooklyn, which took place within a few miles of one another.

The Morris-Jumel Mansion, in Upper Manhattan, near Coogan's Bluff (so named for James Coogan who owned the land in the 1880s), was the site of Washington's headquarters for five weeks in fall 1776. On a high promontory, on what is now 160th Street, it is today one of the oldest existing houses in New York City. It was built in 1765, when the area was rural, by Colonel Roger Morris. For many years it was known as Mount Morris, then a 135-acre estate with views of New York Harbor and New Jersey. The colonel and his wife, Mary Philipse, were Loyalists, however, and they abandoned their home just before the Revolution. In 1810 it was purchased by Stephen Jumel, a wine merchant, and his wife, Eliza, who made a number of alterations.

I'd lived in New York for thirty-five years before I visited this landmark. One August afternoon I decided to remedy that. I took the subway from West Fifty-seventh Street, where I have an art studio, to West 157th (exactly a hundred blocks north), which is the closest stop to the destination. On arriving at the train platform, I saw a small tablet embedded in the tile wall: MORRIS-JUMEL MANSION, WASHINGTON'S HEADQUARTERS. Its worn stone looked as if it had been there since the subway opened, in 1906. None of the commuters jostling past seemed to notice it.

Emerging onto Broadway, I came to a busy corner, where I paused to get my bearings. I stood near the neo-Gothic Church of the Intercession, which takes up a city block and looks more like a cathedral than a church. Across the way, I could see Audubon Terrace, which houses the Hispanic Society and the American Academy of Arts and Letters. In the 1700s, wealthy New Yorkers built summer homes here.

I had made plans to meet Fred Cookinham, a licensed tour guide who earlier had given me a tour of Alexander Hamilton's house. It was now noon, and Fred showed up right on time. He was to give me a private viewing of Morris-Jumel, which he knows well.

Luckily, I'd brought a notebook, because Fred packs a lot of information in a few sentences. He began our tour by telling me that we were standing on hallowed ground. "This area of Manhattan was the site of three military trenches the Patriots used in the Revolutionary War," he said. "If the front ones fell, they had another one to back them up, and then another." According to Fred, we were just above the second one. This was the kind of precise detail he was known for, and it fascinated me. He reached into his bag and pulled out several historical maps, some of which were laminated and tattered at the edges. They showed the exact locations of the trenches, colored by hand with a yellow highlighter. There were other notations in fluorescent pink, reserved for troop movements, forts, and the local topography.

Fred pointed west, toward the Hudson River. "Take a look over there," he said, "where 144th Street falls steeply down to the edge of the island. This is one of highest points of elevation in Manhattan and would have given Washington's troops a clear sightline to the British movements." Buildings now block most of that view, but I could still see a sliver of the Hudson.

"It's hard sometimes to tell the difference in terrain," said Fred, "but you'll notice it when we start walking farther uphill . . ."

Fred folded his maps, wiped the sweat from his forehead, and headed onward. I followed close behind, trying to keep pace. We passed several nineteenth-century brownstones and then we were on St. Nicholas Avenue. The sun beat down, just as it likely would have when the rebels were on the march some 243 years ago. "This street was once called Kingsbridge Road," Fred told me, "because it led to the northern end of Manhattan, where a wooden bridge, the Kings Bridge, crossed into Westchester."

We came to a row of clapboard houses, which looked out of place next to the neighboring brick and limestone structures.

Each of the wood-frame homes had a stoop with an overhang above the front door. "This is Sylvan Terrace," Fred said, "and was built in the 1880s. It's landmarked, and the houses go for more than a million now. They border what was once the front carriage drive of Morris-Jumel."

At the entrance to the mansion, I felt as if I had stumbled onto a Georgia plantation. The white building had two tiers of columns, a portico, and a triangular pediment that looked very neo-Classical. There was a green, sloping lawn with mature trees and a garden. I saw about twenty children running among the bushes, and a few others were sitting on the front steps. "This is a city park," Fred said. "The local community has public access. Nowadays, it's kind of a playground."

The plot was modest, maybe two or three acres, a far cry from what it once was. Nineteenth-century prints show the farm-land and hills that made up the full expanse of the old prop-erty. The exterior of the house now looked somewhat tired and decayed—like Jefferson's Monticello after the Civil War. The paint on Morris-Jumel was chipped in places, and I noticed rotting wood at the base.

Despite this deferred maintenance, there was something proud about Morris-Jumel's appearance. It was stately. At the front of the house, at the second story, there was a balcony with a carved balustrade. I imagined the Morris family admiring their land from this prospect, and I thought of Washington, with spyglass in hand, keeping an eye on British maneuvers in Lower Manhattan.

"Washington supposedly had a study in the back of the house," Fred said. "It's shaped like an octagon. There's a small display there now with a desk, reading spectacles, and a colonial uniform. None of them is authentic, but they do give a sense of the era."

Fred and I entered through the wide front door of the mansion into the first-floor foyer. The furnishings were shabby and antique-looking, although not original. There was a large parlor toward the back, and portraits of the Morris family hung in gilded frames. A series of low-springing arches imparted a sense of grandeur. The walls were covered in patterned wallpaper. "The nonprofit foundation here researched old patterns in Paris, [where the wallpaper originally came from]," said Fred, "to create an historically accurate decor. There's a dedicated group who want this museum to continue and thrive. They've raised a good deal of donations. I've got great admiration for what they're doing."

A small gift shop is to the left of the entrance. There you'll find books, postcards, and bobbleheads of Washington. I bought a small volume on the history of the house, by Carol S. Ward, hoping to increase the coffers. Maintaining an old house is a money pit; few days go by without a burst pipe, a cracking wall, or a leaky roof.

I started thumbing through my new book and immediately learned a few things. Aaron Burr had a connection to the house. Eliza Bowen Jumel, a widow and the last owner of the home, married him late in his life—fifteen years after he had killed Hamilton in the duel. He was a pariah by then and perennially in debt. Eliza soon realized that he was after her fortune and divorced him after a year. In the front hall is a portrait of her, sitting in a chair surrounded by her grandchildren. According to one of the brochures, her ghost haunts the house.

As Fred and I were leaving the mansion, he told me an interesting story about Washington: When he was president, fourteen years after he had made his headquarters here, Washington returned to Morris-Jumel. In July 1790, he arranged a dinner for his Cabinet in this then-pastoral setting. Among the guests were Vice President John Adams, Alexander Hamilton, Henry Knox, and Thomas Jefferson, who was secretary of state. There's no transcript of what they said over dinner, but the discussions were presumably not about conducting a war but rather about preserving the peace.

Every year the mansion commemorates this meeting of the Founding Fathers. A period-inspired multicourse dinner is served to visitors. I pulled out my notebook and put the date on my calendar for the following year. This time I would go without Fred—but thanks to him, I was now ready to conduct my own tour.

A Final Plea

BILLOP HOUSE (CONFERENCE HOUSE)
Staten Island, New York

I'M ONE of those Manhattanites who rarely visit the city's four other boroughs. It's a sign, I admit, of a certain provincialism, I think. Recently, however, I've become more adventurous. In June, 2018, I went to Staten Island, where I discovered one of the more significant landmarks of the Revolution.

Billop House or, as it's formally known, the Conference House, is about as far away from Manhattan as you could possibly go and still be in the Big Apple. The old building is at the southernmost tip of Staten Island, in Tottenville, and it sits peacefully on a grassy knoll overlooking Raritan Bay.

On September 11, 1776, shortly after the Battle of Brooklyn—a devastating defeat for Washington—Benjamin Franklin, John Adams, and Edward Rutledge (a member of the Continental Congress, from South Carolina) met here with Admiral Richard Howe, of the British navy. Howe and his brother General William Howe were co-commanders in chief of North America, and had convinced the king to name them both peace commissioners, thereby giving them the authority to negotiate a settlement and grant a pardon to any American who returned to royal allegiance. Richard used Billop House to quarter his officers and had arranged a conference there in hopes of persuading the Americans to renounce independence and agree to a diplomatic solution.

Three Patriots stood their ground in this stone house in Staten Island

The three emissaries from the Congress listened to Howe's proposal but were unmoved. They respectfully declined the olive branch, even after they were promised full pardons—and a reprieve from the gallows for what amounted to treason. Franklin said, with steely resolve, that the die was cast: the Declaration had been signed, there was no turning back. Given that the British army and naval forces far outnumbered the Americans, it seems that these Patriots were taking a huge risk. But there was little more for Howe to say. The Americans finished their mutton and wine, bade goodbye, and returned to Philadelphia. The Revolution would continue for seven more years.

There are very few extant structures left in New York that you can say with certainty the Founding Fathers have visited. Billop is one of them. And it's not a replica, at least the main structure isn't. I called up my friend Chip Fisher to see if he wanted join me on an excursion. Chip, a connoisseur of all things New York, offered to drive us. We left from Midtown on a Saturday morning, when traffic would be light.

Zooming south in Chip's sporty sedan, we made good time on the FDR Drive and the Verrazzano-Narrows Bridge. It was no surprise that Chip, who has walked Manhattan top to bottom, knew the bridge's history. "The Verrazzano was once the longest suspension bridge in America," he said. "Gay Talese wrote a book about it. He describes it as a masterpiece of engineering and talks about the Italian workers who built it. I remember seeing it go up as a kid in the sixties."

Exiting the ramp on the other side of the bridge, Chip stopped the car to point to the sign for Fort Wadsworth. "It's a slight detour but worth going sometime," he said. "The fort goes back to the Dutch in the 1600s and was later rebuilt during the Civil War. But because New York was never attacked, it wasn't used much other than as a garrison for federal troops during the Draft Riots [July 1863] in Manhattan."

Back in gear, Chip and I rode along Route I-278, which crosses the length of Staten Island. We passed stretches of warehouses and other industrial buildings before the GPS landed us at our destination, 7455 Hyland Boulevard. A sign for the Conference House was visible across the street from where we'd parked. Nearby, several modest homes were packed close together. We got out of the car, passed through a wooden gate, and made our way down to the water.

There was a small sandy beachfront amid some overgrown, weedy brush. Chip and I watched as the tiny waves rippled to shore. We turned around and headed up to the house, trying to imagine the events of that day nearly 250 years ago when the Americans could have have lost faith and retreated from their plans for independence.

Franklin, Adams, and Rutledge supposedly landed by boat after staying overnight in Patriot-held Perth Amboy, New Jersey. (There's an amusing story about Adams and Franklin sharing a bed at a tavern, in which they argued all night about whether or not their windows should be left open.) Disembarking, the three men were "greeted" by a row of Hessian soldiers who lined the entryway to the house—a show of force that likely didn't intimidate the Patriots, who had been promised by Howe that they would not be captured.

The Conference House is constructed of multicolored field-stone with white-trimmed windows and is framed by a couple of mature trees. A set of wooden steps lead to the front door. We were met in the entry hall by an elderly couple who were sitting on small chairs, listening intently to a radio.

"Are you waiting for the tour guides to arrive?" I said, assuming they were history seekers like ourselves.

"No, we're your tour guides," the woman said. "You're the

first visitors today. Sorry about the radio; we were just catching a college football game."

"Who's playing?" I asked.

"Ithaca versus Cortland. Ithaca is up fourteen to seven."

She introduced herself. "I'm Bonnie and this is Jerry. I'll start you off in the main rooms and then he'll take you down to the basement."

She gave us a little, more-recent history: "First off," she began, "let me tell you that in the 1920s this place was about to be bulldozed, but a group of concerned citizens got together to save it and have the city buy it. It was a wreck. Here's a photo of what the people looked like who fought to preserve the place." She handed us a postcard with a black-and-white image of well-heeled men and women sitting on the front stoop.

Bonnie then pointed us in the direction of the front parlor, where Howe had conducted the conference: "Howe's senior officers were stationed in the house," she said. "Howe mostly stayed overnight at a tavern in town. There's a painting in the front hall that gives you an idea of what the British looked like, dressed in wigs and breeches."

The furniture in the handsome room consisted of a set of antique tables and chairs and a Dutch armoire with a broad cornice. None of the pieces was original. "The only authentic item is the sea chest owned by the Billop family, but the historical society has worked hard to get substitute pieces from the eighteenth century," Bonnie said. "The Billops were Tories and took a lot of their stuff when they escaped."

The long shadows of late afternoon filtered through the windows, which had thick mullions. Chip noticed the panes. "See the wavy lines?" he asked. "This is clearly old glass."

As we walked across the hall to the dining room, we saw a large fireplace and portraits of the Billops' ancestors.

"Would you like to see the upstairs?" Bonnie asked.

We followed her up ("Watch your head!") the narrow steps to the second-story landing. There were two bedrooms, one of which had a four-poster bed with hanging drapery and small-scale desks for children to sit at. In the other room was a spinning wheel.

Back downstairs, we found Jerry waiting to take us to the scullery on the ground level. He was still listening to the radio. "How's the game going?" I asked.

"Ithaca is winning, but it's only the third quarter. There's a lot of time left."

We followed Jerry down a set of rickety wooden steps, which the servants once had to use to get to and from the kitchen. The kitchen had a wide fireplace with a Dutch oven (for baking bread), several heavy cast-iron pots, and a bellows. "Look at the ceiling," Jerry said, pointing to the beams above us: "Red oak from first-growth trees. Hand hewn. You can see some of the old flat nails still sticking out of them."

Jerry drew our attention to an array of bricks on the floor. They were arranged in a distinctive pattern. "These are ballast bricks," he said. "They were originally used on clipper ships to balance the weight. When the ships docked and the cargo was unloaded, the crew put the bricks in the hold. The leftover bricks were often used to pave streets. They called them cobblestones."

"What's the insignia stamped on them?" I asked.

"That was the trademark of the company that restored them, using the original molds. They're from Holland," Jerry explained. "Notice that the bricks have three distinct colors: orange, blue, and white. Guess why?"

"Flag of the Netherlands?" I guessed, summoning my distant Dutch ancestry.

"Yep!" said Jerry. "The queen of the Netherlands came here

on a ceremonial visit in 1929, when the final brick was set in place on the floor of this room. New York, I knew, was once called New Amsterdam.

"Follow me over here to the root cellar," he continued. "This is where they stored the vegetables. It was the first room they built after the foundation was laid. Workers filled a pit in the ground with sand from the shoreline and then laid the bricks on top to form this vault. Pretty ingenious, huh?"

As the tour wound down, I asked Jerry about himself. "I grew up on Staten Island, not far from here," he said. "Bonnie is from upstate New York. I used to sell auto parts. Now I'm retired and do this tour-guide thing as a volunteer. It's interesting work."

We made our way back up the narrow basement staircase, which was sized for a dollhouse, and found Bonnie in the hall, adjusting the radio dial.

"Is the game over?" I asked.

"Almost. Ithaca just missed a field goal. They have a stinky kicker," she said.

During the Battle of Princeton, Nassau Hall was used as a British garrison.

Turning the Tide

I N A large open field in Princeton, New Jersey, near the Institute for Advanced Study, a huge oak tree stood for some
three hundred years. Its trunk was close to eight feet in
diameter and its heavy branches were almost half as thick. In
its old age, locals diligently kept it alive by pruning it regularly.
In 2000, after a violent windstorm, the tree finally gave way. The
loss of such a natural wonder was sad. But for those who know
their history, there was another reason to mourn: It was at the
base of this oak that a Revolutionary War hero, General Hugh
Mercer, was killed.

Mercer was one of George Washington's most trusted generals. At the Battle of Princeton, in January 1777, with the British closing in, he refused to abandon his men, even after being mortally wounded. In honor of Mercer, who was originally
from Scotland and fought on the British side in the Seven Years'
War, the tree was christened the Mercer Oak. For many years
it has been the symbol on the town seal. Thanks to Princeton's
historical commission, a new tree now sits on that site, planted
with an acorn salvaged from the original.

I was not aware of this story until my friend Jack Kerr told
it to me one afternoon at the University Club in New York.
Jack was interested in my book project and offered to give me

a tour of the battlefield. He happens to live in Princeton—on Mercer Road—and along with being a law partner at Simpson Thatcher and Bartlett in New York, he's an avid amateur historian. We picked a date in early fall 2019.

I took a train from Manhattan to Princeton Junction, and Jack picked me up at the station. "I thought I'd give you the lay of the land before we hit the battlefield," he said.

I'd just finished buckling my seatbelt when Jack began: "It's important to remember why the Battle of Princeton was so significant. Washington and his army were struggling at the time. In late 1776 they'd lost the Battles of Brooklyn, Fort Washington, and White Plains—in quick succession—and were now being chased all over New Jersey by Cornwallis. Luckily, they'd scored a victory at Trenton the day after Christmas that year, after Washington crossed the Delaware. So morale was a bit higher than it might have been. Washington's victory at Princeton, at this early stage of the war, kept the momentum going, though I'm biased after living here for so many years. It was one of the first times the Americans won a real battle in the open field. The earlier victory at Trenton against the Hessians was major, but it wasn't a typical engagement. It was basically a surprise raid on an enemy camp."

As we drove down Nassau Street, we passed the Princeton University campus. Jack lowered his window and pointed out one of the main buildings. "There's Nassau Hall," he said. "At one time that building was the entire college. It was the largest structure in the colonies and was constructed like a fortress. The British were garrisoned here, and legend has it that Alexander Hamilton's artillery shot a cannonball through one of the windows, knocking down a portrait of George III."

Jack drove on another mile and then stopped near a monument, a stone sculpture of Washington in full uniform. Jack pulled out some books from the backseat. They were dog-eared with handwritten notes sandwiched between the pages. I was impressed with the research he'd done for our little tour, and told him so.

"I majored in history at Boston College," Jack said. "I've read a lot about the Revolution, so this is fun for me."

We got out of the car and walked to the monument. It's set at the end of an allée of trees and stands more than twenty feet high. It was sculpted by Frederick MacMonnies and was dedicated in 1922 by President Warren Harding. Washington is depicted standing among a group of soldiers. One of them is Mercer. I took some photos with my phone, then we headed back onto Stockton Street (named after Richard Stockton, a signer of the Declaration, who lived in a house nearby).

Our next stop was a trailhead at the edge of a forest just outside of town. "I'd like to take you on a walking path through these woods," said Jack. "It's part of the historic route that Washington's army took on the way to the Princeton battle-field." When the forest opened up and we came out onto a sunny expanse, Jack directed my attention to an old house in the clearing. It had white clapboards with eight-over-eight windows and stood beside ancient locust trees.

"Here's where the fighting began," Jack said. "This is the Clarke House, right smack in the middle of it. The Clarke family wasn't expecting war on their doorstep, but that's what happened. Both sides were marching in opposite directions near here, but they accidentally bumped into each other and the Clarkes were caught in the crossfire."

We knocked at the back door. "Welcome, good timing!" said Will Krakower, education director of the house. "I was just about to close up for lunch. Let me take you around."

He started our tour at a small exhibit near the foyer called *The*

IN THE FOUNDERS' FOOTSTEPS

Arms of the Revolution. It contained firearms as well as a repro-
duction of a painting of the Princeton battle by James Peale, a
member of the famous Peale family of artists. In it both armies
are firing at one another from behind rows of cattle fences.
Peale, like one of his brothers, was a soldier. "Because Peale
was actually a member of the Continentals," Will said, "we can
assume his rendering is pretty accurate. Look how close the
armies are to each other—no more than fifty yards. That's about
as far as a musket ball could fly. It wasn't exactly hand-to-hand
combat, but it was close."

Will, who studied history at Rutgers, then led us past a country kitchen, which had several culinary implements on display,
including heavy round pots and long iron ladles. The fireplace,
surrounded by raised-panel walls, was capacious; it had to ac-
commodate a full day of cooking. I could almost smell fatty
beef simmering under the heat of slow-burning logs.

As we headed up a narrow staircase to the second floor, Will
told us he'd been working at the site for some two years, and
that he'd been a guide at the Washington Crossing Historic
Park, in Pennsylvania. "We get about ten thousand visitors a
year at the Clarke House," he said, "which is pretty good for a
historic site that isn't that well known."

At the top of the landing, the old plaster walls gave off a
dank, musty smell. "This bedroom," Will said, pointing to a
small chamber with a four-poster, "is where Mercer died. He
was brought in from the battlefield and after several days suc-
cumbed to his wounds. Dr. Benjamin Rush, who was a signer of
the Declaration, was in attendance but was unable to save him.
Mercer was a highly experienced field commander, so his loss
was devastating."

At the end of our visit, Will showed us a small watercolor
by John Trumbull, another artist-soldier, which was hanging

inside a glass case. "Trumbull came here after the war to make studies of the site so that he could complete his large painting *The Death of Mercer*," he said. That picture now hangs in the Yale Art Gallery, and I learned later that Trumbull posed Hugh's son for the image of his father.

Jack and I headed back to the car. "How about lunch?" Jack suggested. "I'll take you to the Advanced Study's cafeteria. The food is quite good." The dining hall is located in a sixties-style cast-cement building and was a bit of culture shock after wandering through the eighteenth century. But I was hungry, and happy to get something to eat.

Jack filled me in about the Institute: "It was founded by the Bambergers, the New Jersey department store family, in the 1930s, as a place to invite primarily Jewish-refugee scholars to do research. Einstein was one of them."

After lunch, Jack took me back to the station and I caught the 6:20 bound for New York. As I sat looking out the window, I pondered the battle's pivotal moment: It gave the Continental Army the confidence that it could win.

The road to independence began with oysters soaked in buttermilk.

A Taste of History

CITY TAVERN · *Philadelphia, Pennsylvania*

O N JULY 4, 1777, America celebrated its first year of independence. It was the cause for much jubilation and flag waving. But if one were to guess where the inaugural festivities were held, most likely the answer wouldn't be a tavern. Yet a tavern it was: City Tavern in Philadelphia. In those days, such establishments were more than simple watering holes. There were no office buildings, stock exchanges, or banks, so taverns often served these functions. They were also gathering places to plot revolutions.

For the Founding Fathers, City Tavern was a safe haven. In 1774 Paul Revere came here to deliver the latest news from Boston. That same year, delegates from the Continental Congress convened here after sessions in nearby Carpenters' Hall. In 1777, after the outbreak of the Revolution, Washington met Lafayette here. The Continental Army used the tavern as its headquarters. And in 1789, the tavern was the site of a banquet for Washington as he traveled from Philadelphia to New York to be sworn in as president.

With so much history, it's difficult to believe that this landmark was pretty much forgotten for more than a hundred years. After a fire in 1834, it lay in shambles; in 1854 it was finally razed. It would take authorization from Congress, in 1948, to make plans to restore it. And it would take another twenty-five years before a replica was completed. It officially opened in 1976, for the Bicentennial.

For the next eighteen years, the "new" tavern tried to make a go of it. But it was a sleepy place that relied on a fickle seasonal clientele. The menu was ordinary and the food equally so. In 1994, though, a chef—and a European one at that—was hired. Walter Staib, then in his forties and well traveled, brought a new culture and mission to City Tavern. He sought to revive its rich legacy and restore its traditions. Staib introduced dishes from the colonial era, repapered the walls to reflect eighteenth-century tastes, dressed the waiters in period attire, and installed authentic-looking furniture, such as trestle tables and Windsor chairs.

The hard work paid off and the tavern's reputation grew steadily. Today it's a popular destination for tourists. They can step back in time and sample the same fare that Jefferson and Adams dined on. They can also meet chef Walter, who has since become a celebrity. He hosts the Emmy Award–winning PBS series *A Taste of History*, which is based on the recipes he prepares for the restaurant.

"I knew very little about American history when I began," Walter told me when I visited the tavern in 2019. "But I started educating myself and found the old stories intriguing. One in particular I recall: When John Adams came to attend the first Continental Congress, in August 1774, the prominent leaders in town brought him here and showed him such a good time that he would remember the place as 'the most genteel tavern in America.'"

Walter Staib looks like a chef. He's portly, but he carries the extra weight well. He has a neatly trimmed white beard and keen eyes. He was wearing a white chef's coat with buttons across the chest. There were a few stains on it, evidence he'd been working in the kitchen.

My friend Bob Demento, who accompanied me on this visit, had made the introductions. Bob knows everyone who's anyone in Philly. "Walter's a fount of knowledge," he told me.

While Walter talked more about the tavern's past, including the fact that it held British prisoners during the Revolution, he was showing us to our table. It was in a cozy corner in the front room next to a fireplace. A bubbly cranberry spritzer in a tall glass was waiting for each of us.

Bob and I perused the menu: Would we have lobster pie with sherry cream sauce, braised rabbit with egg noodles, or crab cakes with herbed remoulade? "No need to place an order," the chef said. "I've arranged a special lunch for you."

On cue, a waiter in tan breeches and a long white shirt with frills on the cuffs brought in a tray of fried oysters. They were topped with a light, flaky cornbread crust and sprinkled with pepper.

"This was a favorite of Washington's," said Walter. "He loved oysters soaked in buttermilk."

Next came a plate of thick toast smothered in hollandaise sauce with crispy bacon. "Now you're eating what Jefferson liked," the chef said. He left to greet another guest.

Bob and I tucked in. We were scooping up the remains of the rich gravy when another dish arrived: pepperpot soup in a hot skillet when Walter returned. "The soldiers ate this in the field before crossing the Delaware," he said. "It was quick and easy to make, and combined beef with taro and habernero peppers."

"Is all your food made on the premises?" I asked.

"Yes, we use an ancient fire oven for cooking, which gives the food an authentic taste. Now, how about a glass of wine?" Bob and I showed no hesitation.

"Here's one that was popular with Jefferson," the chef told us. "He developed a taste for it in Paris while he was ambassador to France. He brought back seeds from Bordeaux and planted them in a trough so they would survive the ocean crossing on his return. There's a vineyard, Barton & Guestier, where he went, and it still makes the wine. At the time, southern French wines were looked down upon. But Jefferson changed people's minds. While he was president, he ordered hundreds of bottles of it."

Bob and I each drank a glass and then leaned back in our chairs, stuffed. Walter was happy to see that we were full. There's no better compliment to a chef than an empty plate.

As we waited for the next course, Walter told us about himself: "I was born in Germany," he said, "in Pforzheim. I had some chefs in my family and I worked for them from an early age. I bounced around at various jobs in Switzerland, Brazil, and Chicago."

Walter, who had been standing, finally pulled up a chair. He continued: "One of my breaks was as a sous-chef. I then worked in a luxury resort on the Italian border, on Lago Maggiore. All these jobs gave me great experience. They prepared me for City Tavern."

He paused for a moment and looked out the window. Thick pine green drapes were tied back against its frame; they matched the pine green of the linens on each of the round tables. "I've enjoyed my time here," he said. "It was a challenge at first, but I worked with National Parks Service curator Karie Diethorn, who helped me select the proper silverware, furnishings, paint colors, and linens."

As we got ready to leave, after having finished a dessert of vanilla bean crème brulee, I asked the chef what his next project was.

"I'm planning for my upcoming TV segment a trip to Malverne, not far from here, where the Revolutionary Battle of

Paoli—just outside of Philadelphia—was fought. I'm working on what they would have eaten there: braised short ribs and Pennsylvania Dutch gratin. But I hope to learn of other recipes as well. You never know what I might discover."

As for me, I'd already made a great discovery: a tavern with an extraordinary history, not only of food but also of the Founding Fathers.

Musket shells were no match for the thick stone walls of Cliveden.

House of War

CLIVEDEN MANOR (THE CHEW HOUSE)
Germantown, Pennsylvania

THE BATTLE of Germantown is remembered for many things but not, I suspect, for a dog. Oddly enough, though, a canine played a memorable role. It wasn't because the animal affected the outcome but instead because it shed light on those who fought. The tale is at once touching and a head-scratcher.

To set the stage: In September 17, 1777, after victories at Brandywine and Paoli, the British occupied Philadelphia. Their army quartered in the village of Germantown, a few miles north of the city. That October, George Washington plotted a strategy to regain Philadelphia, using the element of surprise that had been so successful at Trenton. Departing from his base in Skippack, Pennsylvania (Montgomery County), during the early morning of October 4, Washington mobilized twelve thousand men and split them into separate groups heading toward Germantown, each using a different byway. Washington's own column marched through Chestnut Hill and Mount Airy but was compromised. A Redcoat soldier spotted the Patriots and alerted Colonel Thomas Musgrave, whose Fortieth Regiment was stationed near Cliveden Manor.

As the Americans advanced toward Germantown, Musgrave mobilized his men to garrison at the manor, barricading the doors and shuttering the windows. The heavy stone walls, unusual at a time when houses were usually constructed of wood, helped convert the mansion into a fortress. The American artillery proved futile against its impenetrable walls. Cannonballs barely dinged them; musket balls managed only to chip the masonry. Staked at the second story, the British fired, easily picking off the rebels in the open air below. The rebels made attempts to set fire to the house with torches, but waiting British bayoneted them from cellar windows.

Some 150 Americans died and 520 were wounded (with 412 missing), many just a few feet from the front door. Several notable Patriot officers were engaged in the conflict, including Nathanael Greene, Lord Stirling, and "Mad" Anthony Wayne (so-called for his stormy personality). After the fight—which lasted three hours—the Hessian captain John Ewald described Cliveden as looking "like a slaughterhouse." The American artist Howard Pyle would later paint his imagined view of the carnage (*Scribner's* magazine, 1897), showing men scarred and bloodied on the doorstep.

The Americans, thus beaten back, would eventually retreat to Montgomery County and then to Valley Forge for the winter. If there was one consolation in their defeat, it was that the world took notice of how hard they fought. The *London Chronicle* reported: "To do the rebels justice, they attacked with great intrepidity."

But let's step back for a moment and return to the dog. As the tale goes, General Howe, commander of the British forces, owned a hound (the exact breed not known) that accompanied him on his campaigns. But at Germantown, Howe's dog got loose and crossed enemy lines during the battle. When Washington discovered it the following day, wandering among the wounded soldiers, he saw that the dog's collar read G. HOWE.

Washington summoned one of his men to carry a white flag and return the animal to its rightful owner, with a note penned by his aide-de-camp Alexander Hamilton: "General Washington's compliments to General Howe. He does himself the pleasure to return [to] him a dog, which accidentally fell into his hands, and by the inscription on the collar appears to belong to General Howe."

What prompted this gesture by Washington? Most likely it was an act of chivalry. Officers in the eighteenth century followed a code of honor and duty, even as enemies. It was not uncommon, for example, to invite a defeated general to dinner following a battle—as was the case at Yorktown after the British surrendered. And when Benedict Arnold requested his clothes be returned to him following his defection (he had forgotten them in his haste to escape West Point), Washington complied.

I first visited Cliveden in June 2019. My friend Bob Demento arranged a private tour—as he had done for me at Independence Hall—with Carolyn Wallace, the education director. Bob met me in the morning at the Penn's View Hotel in Philadelphia's historic district, where I was staying. We drove out of town on a winding highway, hugging close to the Schuylkill River as Bob pointed out various sites. One was of the location of the old Rittenhouse Paper Mill, one of the largest in the colonies. "Everything was made in Philadelphia during that time," Bob said. "We forget that now, because New York has become the center for everything."

We arrived just before lunch at Germantown, which is now a pleasant suburb with three-story Victorians. During the late 1700s, it was a popular summer retreat for wealthy Philadelphians, particularly during the yellow fever epidemic. Carolyn met us at the entrance.

The house, built in 1763, is impressive in scale, with twelve-over-twelve windows and thick wood mullions. Some classically inspired statuary on the lawn gives the appearance of a mini–English estate. Carolyn said the house was built by the Benjamin Chew family, whose descendants emigrated to America in 1622. Chew was a prominent lawyer who represented William Penn in several land-boundary negotiations. "The Chews' builder used two-foot-thick walls made of local schist," she said, "and based the design on a pattern book by the builder Jacob Noor. Cannonballs actually bounced off the walls, and you can see some original marks where they hit. The Chews and their descendants held on to their homestead for seven generations and kept the house looking the same. Their estate, though, was many more acres than it is today."

I looked around and observed suburban development surrounding the property. Though some mature trees blocked the view of neighboring houses, it was clearly a less private residence than it once was.

The front steps were of marble and worn smooth with age. In the front hall a group of muskets leaned against the wall. "These are examples of the three types that were used during the time," said Carolyn, who has worked at the site since 2014. "The longest one was the Kentucky rifle, which gave better aim. It took most men about sixty seconds to load this gun; a few could do it in half that time." She held up one of the rifles and described how a soldier had to bite off the paper wrapping from the cartridge, and then load the musketball down the barrel. I couldn't help but think of the AK-47s in today's mass shootings, which can fire off a hundred rounds a second.

Moving on to the stair hallway, our guide pointed to an area where the original front doors were once displayed as relics. "They had the old musket holes from when the Americans attacked," she said. "The doors were stored for many years in a nearby carriage shed, but they were destroyed by arson not long ago. It was a 'distraction fire,' set by someone who intended to burn down the nearby church. If you look over here, though," she said, pointing to the stairs, "you can still make out some holes in the wooden railing."

Other rooms were sparsely furnished, as most of the original effects were sold off or damaged over time. A Chippendale armoire in one of the parlors gave an aristocratic air to the interior. Above it was a marble bust of John Locke. On a window ledge was a framed etching of General Musgrave, which seemed strange given that he was on the side of the British.

The upper bedrooms were especially interesting to me. The windows were very big, and they helped me envision the way several soldiers, bunched together, could have fired multiple volleys.

The final room we saw was the kitchen. It had 1950s cabinetry and looked very lived in. "The historical committee wanted to keep the house looking the way it did when the last Chew descendants still lived here," Carolyn told us. "The National Trust for Historic Preservation, which purchased the house in 1972, even contacted the family to get the name of the original refrigerator so it could make sure to replicate the one that broke."

After seven generations in the same family, I think this level of detail—this faithful replication—would have pleased the last Chew descendants to live in this house.

Quaint log cabins at Valley Forge belie the suffering within.

Winter of Discontent

VALLEY FORGE HISTORIC SITE
King of Prussia, Pennsylvania

I F YOU google "George Washington at Valley Forge," chances are you'll come across a picture by Arnold Friberg, painted in 1975. It shows Washington kneeling alone in the snow, his hands clasped in prayer. Washington was a deeply religious man, and it's possible he did, in fact, pray. He certainly had reason to. Some two thousand of his men had died that winter and early spring of 1777–78, many from disease or starvation, in what became a horrific six months. On February 16, 1778, in the midst of the crisis, the general wrote to Governor Clinton, of New York: "For some days past, there has been little less than a famine in camp. A part of the army has been a week without any kind of flesh and rest for three or four days. Naked and starving as they are, we cannot enough admire the incomparable patience and fidelity of the soldiery, that they have not been ere this excited by their sufferings, to a general mutiny or dispersion."

Washington pleaded with Congress for more supplies, but received little for his pains. Congress was hampered by scarcity of money, failure of credit, and an inefficient administrative system mired in bureaucratic wrangling. Meanwhile Washington's army was reeling from a string of defeats in Pennsylvania during spring 1777—at Paoli, Brandywine, and Germantown. Each had been an attempt to win back Philadelphia, a major colonial city, from the British.

Washington could no longer afford to wait for Congress to act. He tried, instead, to purchase food from the locals around Valley Forge, but met with resistance. Farmers would rather sell to the English, whose currency was more valuable. Furthermore, some of these farmers were reluctant because of their Loyalist leanings. Why support a fight against people who had the same language, religion, and customs? Pennsylvania, like New York and most of the South, had a sizable population that sided with the Crown. In desperation, Washington was forced to confiscate food supplies from the neighboring residents, something he felt morally opposed to.

Given these hardships at Valley Forge, then, how did the Continental Army stay together? And how did the men continue to fight? In the fall of 2019, I set out to find some answers. Traveling by car, I headed out of New York City toward Valley Forge National Park. The address on my navigation system read 1400 North Outer Line Drive, King of Prussia, PA. I took I-95 South through New Jersey and into Pennsylvania. For much of the drive, the only scenery seemed to be numbing stretches of smokestacks and oil storage tanks. The interstate was bumper-to-bumper; fumes were sickening. When I finally got near the Park, I was confronted with shopping malls and high-rise developments. This was not what I expected from my "scenic" tour. It reminded me of the car trips over the years on New York's Route 22, which has widened more and more and transformed from a quiet country roadway to one of stoplight junctions and fast food chains.

Things changed, however, as soon as I passed through the gates of Valley Forge. White lines and exit ramps gave way to the beauty of open fields, mature trees, and stone walls. Wooden fence posts lined the narrow, curving roads.

I arrived at the visitor center and made a beeline for the reception desk. I was told to contact Park Ranger Bill Troppman, who'd been assigned to give me a private tour at three o'clock. The office assistant wrote down his cell number for me, and I called him. "I'm running a little late," Bill said. "I was just firing muskets near one of the cabins." Perfect, I thought, I'm in the right place.

While I waited for him, I looked around the gift shop. There were a number of glossy history books on the shelves (tchotchkes, too, such as Christmas ornaments of Valley Forge snowflakes and Minutemen). One book I skimmed described a "gentlemenly" understanding between officers during the Revolution not to fight in the severe cold. It also detailed how Washington, in addition to Valley Forge, had set up winter camps at Morristown, New Jersey, during the winters of 1778–79 and 1780–81. These were places for the armies to tend to their wounded and regain their strength for the spring campaigns.

As I returned the book to the shelf, I spotted a figure in the shop who had just arrived, dressed in a brown-and-green uniform. It was Bill, a big man with thick white hair, broad shoulders, and a husky voice. He reminded me of a football coach.

"Sorry to keep you," he said. "I was changing out of my soldier's clothes. I was doing a reenactment for a school group. Let's hop in my car."

It was a late November afternoon, but Bill assured me we would get in as much of the tour as possible before evening set in. We climbed into his white SUV just as it began to drizzle, and wove through the park's serpentine byways.

"This area was originally established by Quakers in the 1740s," Bill told me. "They founded the Mount Joy Forge here and formed a small industrial community. Over time, they expanded the ironworks and built mills and houses. The surrounding acreage was rich farmland for growing wheat, Indian corn, hay, and rye. Washington's quartermaster Thomas Mifflin scouted this area near the Schuylkill River and decided it was a good place to camp because it was secluded between two hills."

Our first stop was a row of log cabins. "These were built by the soldiers themselves on Washington's orders," Bill said. "There was prize money for the best ones. Construction began immediately upon arrival at the camp on December 19, 1777, because the troops had no barracks to sleep in and winter had set in. The men grew up on farms in New England, so they knew how to build things. They made the chimneys out of wood, because it was too labor intensive to make stone ones. Originally there were hundreds of these cabins, in long rows. We have ten replicas on display."

We entered one of the cabins. A fire was crackling in the hearth and a soldier, dressed in a blue-and-white uniform with brass buttons, stood next to it. He was holding a musket on his shoulder. "Martin, here, has kindly taken my place so I could meet with you," Bill said.

I eyed the bunk beds and the dirt floor. The room was dark and damp. The exposed walls were caked with mud and straw (waddle and daub) to keep out the draft. There were no windows. Poor air circulation, I learned, led to stuffy, often foul-smelling spaces that were ripe for spreading disease. The latrines were often inadequate.

"You can imagine how many trees were cut down for these cabins," Bill went on. "They were built to house some eleven thousand soldiers. There were about twelve men per cabin, each about fourteen by sixteen. They also needed wood to keep the bake ovens running. There were thousands of loaves of bread needed a day to feed the soldiers."

He spoke passionately about the history of Valley Forge. The rebel army had been in dire need of basic necessities like blankets, he said, and the desertion rate was close to twenty percent. He talked about the meager rations, often just watery soup made from bone marrow. Sometimes the men boiled fat.

In 2019, Bill had been working at Valley Forge for twenty-seven years. "I was a high school teacher for ten years before that," he said. "It takes a lot of training to be a ranger. The National Parks requires us, in addition to our history education, to be peace officers. That means instruction on using firearms, driving emergency vehicles, and arrest techniques. In between my hours here, I'm writing a book on Benjamin Franklin. I have a couple of chapters left."

Back in the car, we continued on our tour. At one point, we stopped and parked to look at a statue of "Mad" Anthony Wayne, who fought at Camden, Yorktown, and Stony Brook, among other battles. At Valley Forge he was revered as a venerable officer, known for his relentless pursuit of the enemy on the battlefield. "His spark of daring might flame into rashness," Washington once wrote, "but it was better to have such a leader and occasionally to cool him than forever to be heating the valor of men who feared they would singe their plooms in battle."

The statue of Wayne on horseback stands on a pink granite base in a large field near some trees. "Look closely," Bill said. "He's facing toward the house where he lived, which is not too far from here. He was more sophisticated than people give him credit for. He was a great reader of history, like his fellow officer Nathanael Greene. He carried around a copy of Caesar's *Gallic Wars* in his pocket."

Another stop was to see the Patriots of African Descent Monument. It is also a granite block with a bronze bas-relief of three Black soldiers, each holding a musket. Erected in 1993, it had been proposed by Martha Russell, a founding member of the Valley Forge Alumnae Chapter. She'd been inspired by a book by Charles Blockson (*Pennsylvania's Black History*, 1975), who discovered that there were no monuments to Black soldiers at Valley Forge. The First Rhode Island Regiment, part of General James Varnum's brigade, included many African Americans as well as Native Americans. Bill Troppman mentioned Thomas Fleming, who uncovered pension records of certain individuals, among them a slave, Samual Surphen, of the New Jersey brigade who had substituted for his master; and Shadrak Battles, a thirty-two-year-old "freeman of color" who enlisted in the 10th Virginia Regiment in 1779. Fleming chronicled his findings in *Washington's Secret War: The Hidden History of Valley Forge* (2005).

Our next stop was George Washington's headquarters: a fieldstone building with white trim, characteristic of the Delaware Valley. Bill pointed out the flag in front: A replica, it had thirteen stars—one for each of the colonies. "This was one of the first flags of the new republic," he said.

"In front of this house, there would have been Washington's elite guards, assigned to protect him," Bill said. "There were about fifty of them, kind of like the Secret Service today. You needed a password before they let you in."

We climbed a set of wooden steps and entered into a hallway with a stairwell. "Washington used this building as his base of operations, but he insisted on paying rent to the Isaac Potts family, who owned it," Bill said. "He was just near enough to the soldiers' cabins to be a presence to them and far enough to have the privacy and quiet he needed to conduct his business. Two of his aides-de-camp, John Laurens and Alexander Hamilton, joined him in residence here. They would have worked in the front room, and the back room was Washington's. It was sort of the Pentagon of its time."

I looked around. Quill pens and parchment paper were laid out, with candles, on the table in one of the parlors. Bill told me it wasn't always easy working with Washington, despite his reputation as calm, cool, and collected. "He could be hot-tempered," Bill said. "He reminds me a lot of Eisenhower, who could have volcanic eruptions. Hamilton once wrote to a fellow officer about his commander: 'The old man is about to blow!'" Bill didn't elaborate, but I had read that Washington was capable of outbursts. At the landing of Kips Bay, in 1776, he was so furious at his fleeing soldiers that he pulled out his horse whip and swiped at them. "Are these the men with which I am to defend America!" he exclaimed.

When we left, Bill and I walked past an old railway station with an overhanging roof, and I asked him what it was used for. "This was built in the early days of the 1900s," he said, "when tourists came here in small railcars, before automobiles." It was too bad, I thought, that the rail was no longer in service: Tour buses today routinely clog the lots outside the park.

Our final destination was another bronze statue, this one of a man in a long cloak and hat standing atop a stone pedestal. "Baron von Steuben," Bill said. "He was an unsung hero of the Revolution. He was a former officer in the Prussian War. Some question whether he was an actual baron; regardless, he had a lot of experience in military maneuvers and drills and had written a manual on the subject. He was hired to teach the ragtag troops how to get in shape."

Bill pointed to a meadow below, overgrown with weeds and brush. "This was the parade grounds where Von Steuben marched his men and showed them off to the French allies and whomever else he wanted to impress. By the time the Americans left Valley Forge for good, in June 1778, the soldiers had been transformed into a disciplined army," he told me.

"Come back again December nineteenth," Bill said. "That's when we do a reenactment of the army entering the camp on the same date in 1777. I dress up sometimes but not every year. I'm getting a bit old for this kind of stuff. I know my time is coming because a third grader came up to me the other day and asked if I'd ever met George Washington. Can you believe it? I said no but that I knew Thomas Jefferson!"

The Great Chain

HUDSON RIVER CHAIN MONUMENT
West Point, New York

AMERICANS ARE known for their ingenuity—New Yorkers especially. Take, for example, the stunning design and construction of both the Brooklyn Bridge and the Empire State Building. The former, designed in 1883 by John R. Roebling, was once the longest suspension bridge in the world, and is still considered an engineering marvel. The Empire State Building, designed in 1930, was at the time the tallest steel skyscraper and, remarkably, went up in just a little more than a year.

Another, lesser-known marvel, just fifty miles north of these structures, was built at the height of the Revolution, during the spring of 1778. It wasn't a bridge or a building: It was an iron chain. Thomas Machin, an engineer, was the brains behind it and his task was to design a barrier that would span the Hudson River—from West Point to Constitution Island—to block British ships from passing through. The Hudson, which stretches from New York Harbor to Troy, was a key corridor dividing the colonies. Whoever controlled the Hudson could split the American defense in half.

The massive chain required sixty tons of iron, and General Washington, who ordered the project, gave Machin only six weeks to fabricate it. An earlier attempt at a chain had been installed farther upstream but it had failed, and this version would have to succeed. The task required imagination and daring, but Machin was ready for it. He had been an apprentice to a canal builder in England and a captain in an artillery company in America.

During the fall of 1776, British frigates had been passing through these waters at will. The Hudson was too wide for the Americans' cannonfire to be effective from the shoreline. A warship needed only to sail straight down the middle to be untouchable. Washington knew this all too well from the failures at Fort Lee and Fort Washington that same year, when those defenses proved useless in stalling the British on the water.

Machin set to work on the Great Chain in late March 1778. The manufacturing was a prodigious undertaking. There were no great iron factories at that time, just small forges fueled by charcoal pits. And the only way the links of chain could be transported was by flatbed sleds. Each hand-forged link weighed more than one hundred pounds. In early spring, the ground was muddy and slippery, making it difficult to maneuver. When they arrived, it took a week for forty men to install the chain. Upon completion, it was heralded as one of the most important contributions to the war.

But let's pause for a moment. Of all the 315-mile stretch of the Hudson, why was West Point chosen? What was so critical about that location?

"West Point was the 'cork in the bottle' on the Hudson," James Johnson, an expert on the Revolution, told me by phone in 2020. "That portion of the river is the narrowest and the hardest to navigate. The wind is unreliable and there's a sort of Venturi effect created by the close proximity of the four hills. The British would've had to slow down before going by and would have had to tack, so it was an ideal position for the Americans to fire on them."

Links of the original chain form a monument above the mighty Hudson.

IN THE FOUNDERS' FOOTSTEPS

Professor Johnson knows of what he speaks. Not only has he taught military history at West Point and Marist College, but he has also sailed the Hudson on a replica of the HMS *Rose* (a twenty-gun ship of the Royal Navy). In addition, he's the proud owner of a copy of one the links of the chain—albeit a wooden one—that was made for the 240th anniversary of its creation, in 2018.

"I have a simple replica of the chain," he told me. "But there's actually still some of the original chain left. Thirteen links are displayed outdoors at West Point at Trophy Point. They're set on a high location with a great view of the Hudson. Machin specified seven hundred and fifty links. Many of them were melted down for ore after the war. They were generally more than a foot long—you get a sense of how big they are from a painting by Mort Kunstler [1994]. He takes some creative license, but it's a dramatic image."

I took a moment to check Google images of the painting. In it, Washington is looking across the Hudson with a spyglass. Parts of the chain are lying on the ground, in a great mass, ready to be assembled.

"The chain was laid across the river on April 30, 1778," the professor went on. "After they tried once, the British never challenged it again. They were impressed by how the Americans pulled it off. The English made one more attack on the Hudson, at Stony Point in 1779, but they went up against 'Mad' Anthony Wayne and were defeated."

James Johnson is a retired member of the armed forces. He served thirty years in the US Army, retiring as a colonel. He commanded two field artillery batteries, one in Germany and the other in Korea. He's also the editor of *Key to the Northern Country: The Hudson River Valley in the American Revolution* (2013).

He recognizes the contributions of engineers during the Revolution: "Thaddeus Kosciuszko, a Polish engineer and general, designed the redoubts at West Point, which were vital defensive posts," he said. "There's a memorial to him at the Academy."

But the professor reserves his highest praise for Thomas Machin. "Machin knew water," he said. "He had the knowledge of how to float the chain across the river and anchor it at either shore. He specified log rafts to support the links. The rafts allowed the chain to be removed during the winter. A wood boom was placed south of the chain to prevent the British from ramming it."

There are differing views on where the iron for the chain was obtained. Some historians believe it came from mines in New Jersey. Others, like Doc Bayne, a historian of the Hudson Valley, believes it came from Sterling Ironworks, in what is now Tuxedo Park, New York. According to Bayne, the iron was smelted in the Sterling Furnace and the pig-iron bars were brought to secret forges to be formed into links. The links were then transported in tens by oxen to New Windsor, New York.

In any case, the chain was American ingenuity at its best. "As such," James Johnson said, "the chain deserves a far more prominent place in the history of the American road to independence."

America's original sin shrouds the legacy of this once-venerable New York estate.

A Dark Past

I T SEEMS that whenever I'm driving back late at night to Manhattan on the Saw Mill River Parkway, I'm often forced to take a detour for construction or flash flooding. Invariably I end up in the village of Sleepy Hollow, and without fail I get hopelessly lost. The narrow, winding roads of this hidden enclave defy GPS and well-meaning street signs. It's as if the Headless Horseman were lurking in the shadows. I'm always relieved when I get back on the highway.

My most recent trip to Sleepy Hollow was towards the end of the afternoon while there was still daylight—no wrong turns or dismembered torsos. It was the winter of 2020 and I was going to visit Philipsburg Manor, a historic house with ties to the American Revolution. When I got to town, I followed Route 9 past the Pocantico River, a tributary of the Hudson. Off in the distance, in the glare of the setting sun, I could just make out the old manor, with its white exterior, center chimney, and gambrel roof. The house did not seem overly large, but it must have been quite grand in its day.

Philipsburg Manor was built in 1693, ten years before its neighbor the Old Dutch Church. The original inhabitant was Frederick Philipse, a wealthy merchant who owned some fifty thousand acres in much of what is now Westchester County. The Philipse family were heavily involved in the shipping industry and the slave trade. Their enterprise ceased only when, during the Revolution, Frederick's descendants became Loyalists and fled the county seat, never to return. The manor house was later used during the Revolutionary War by the British general Sir Henry Clinton as a base of operations.

Until recently, the history of slavery at Philipsburg—the family not only traded slaves, but also owned them—has gone largely unnoticed. This is primarily, I suspect, because most people don't readily connect slavery with the North. New York, in particular, is remembered during the nineteenth century as a safe haven for African Americans because of the Underground Railroad. But slavery did, indeed, exist in New York, until as late as 1827. It was more predominant on Southern plantations than in the Hudson Valley, but that makes the number of slaves (thirty) at Philipsburg all the more striking.

Today the manor, which is open to the public most of the year, has embraced its shrouded legacy. Like many other historic sites, such as Monticello and Mount Vernon, the guides are more than willing to discuss the enslaved people. In fact, they emphasize the subject. Their "tranparency" has roots in a highly publicized exhibition, in 2005, at the New-York Historical Society called *Slavery in New York*. I had attended the opening and remember the disturbing artifacts on display: advertisements for runaway slaves; posters for "Negroes, to be sold"; and a 1644 document granting "half-freedom" to certain slaves—a ploy by the Dutch to grant slaves specific liberties but still forcing them to abide by draconian rules. The slaves agreed to remain in New York, to pay a yearly tax, to return to service when needed, and to accept that their children remained slaves.

Initially, most visitors to Philipsburg Manor take notice only of the historic buildings and the picturesque setting. A long narrow footbridge crosses a wide pond and leads to the compound. A waterwheel is visible at the side of a rustic barn. Tour guides, or interpreters, are dressed in period costume—breeches for men, long skirts for women. Gradually, we learn that the gristmill—still functioning—was operated by enslaved workers who ground the wheat they cultivated into flour. Other implements show how they fabricated butter from the milk produced in the compound. The butter and wheat and other commodities were eventually exported to plantations in the West Indies. From Adolphe Philipse's postmortem inventory, we learn the slaves' names, such as Caeser, Susan, Abigail, Charles, Tom, Sam.

Some of these men and women are now brought to life, as Sandee Brawarsky explained in an article for the *New York Times* (2017), through ongoing reenactments at the manor: "One vignette, 'North and South,' a disturbing dialogue between a Northern slaveholder and the representative of a Southern slaveholder, was recently staged in the barn, surrounded by cows and oxen," she writes. "Michael Lord, senior site manager of Philipsburg Manor, who wrote the vignettes and sometimes acts in them, said that 'it can be difficult to play the nasty characters… but we need to understand and respect the culture, not shy away from its ugly aspects.'"

For some years following the Revolution, Philipsburg Manor was owned by the Beekman family. The property was in receivership in 1940, at which time the Sleepy Hollow Restorations foundation acquired it. John D. Rockefeller donated funds to rebuild it and it opened to the public in 1943. President George W. Bush proclaimed the site a National Monument in 2006. The manor is operated seasonally and is well worth visiting, especially if you combine it with a tour of the historic Hudson Valley. It offers an important and revealing window into the times in which the Founding Fathers lived. And legend has it that Washington was smitten with Mary Philipse, when they were both in their twenties, and when he was in the Virginia militia. Apparently, he was not an eligible enough suitor to win the hand of one whose father was of such wealth and social standing.

The French general keeps watch for enemy ships at the Bay of Newport.

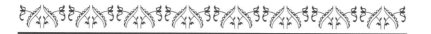

Allies in Arms

O NE OF our nation's most enduring symbols is undoubt-edly the Statue of Liberty. Erected in 1886 to com-memorate the one hundredth anniversary of Ameri-can independence, this colossal sculpture, designed by Frederic Bartholdi, was a gift from France to the people of the United States. Quite a gesture, and one that speaks to an honored bond between these two nations. In recent times, that bond has erod-ed somewhat, but during the American Revolution the alliance forged between France and the colonies was historic and crucial to the formation of this country. Without the French, in short, the Americans would have lost the war for Independence. It was the French alliance that gave the Continental Congress what it desperately needed: a navy, soldiers, and money. Yes, France had ulterior motives. The French despised the English and had been waging war with them for centuries; by aiding America, they could control the balance of power in Europe.

Before the French would open their coffers, however, they needed proof that the Americans could do battle and win. The Saratoga campaign, fought in upstate New York in 1777, was the turning point. America's decisive victory, led by Benedict Arnold and Horatio Gates, showed Louis XVI and his court that the rebels were for real. Benjamin Franklin, Congress's se-cret weapon, did the rest. He spent nearly eight years in Paris as foreign minister—from 1776 to 1783, almost the entirety of the Revolution—and was brilliant at persuading the French to go all in.

But once this alliance was achieved, it was, ironically, the average colonist who needed persuading. To the colonists, the French were a suspect lot (after all, they fought against the Americans in the French and Indian War). In American theaters and newspapers, Frenchmen were depicted as buffoons. According to the historian George Woodbridge, when the French allies, led by General Rochambeau, first arrived in Newport, Rhode Island in July 1780 with fifty-five hundred men, the locals were wary. Woodward writes in a 1980 issue of the *Journal of the Newport Historical Society*: "Rochambeau landed to an unwelcoming Newport. No one received him; shutters and doors were firmly closed. The French believed they had come to help, but the Americans, apparently did not want them. . . . Already the comic stage representation of the Frenchman as a sort of dancing master with dandified manners, with a thin little curled black moustache, reeking of perfume, with effeminate manners, was well established."

Furthermore, the locals remembered only too well that the French had failed them the year before, when they'd promised the colonies (after the formal alliance was established, in the spring of 1778) that they would assist the Rhode Island militia in forcing the British from Newport, which England had occupied since December 1776. Naval Commander General d'Estaing had been dispatched by Louis XVI to aid the effort, but when the general arrived at Newport, a major storm arose. Following various miscommunications, d'Estaing and his army disembarked, leaving the Patriot militia on its own to suffer defeat at the Battle of Rhode Island. The British, who abandoned Newport in October 1779, left the town in a shambles, destroying the fortifications and burning their barracks so nothing could be of use to the enemy.

This unfortunate episode was a sore point for the citizens of Newport. It would take magnanimous gestures by Rochambeau to placate them. After coming ashore (following some three months anchored in the harbor), he offered to pay rent for any land his troops—many of them still sick from the long Atlantic voyage—occupied as campgrounds; and he would pay not in depreciating American currency but in gold and silver coins. Moreover, any supplies he procured he would pay for as well.

It would take a few days for Newport's citizens, many of whom were Loyalists, to warm up to their new "visitors," but gradually Rochambeau's promises allayed suspicion. Eventually, the shutters and doors opened. Washington even sent an ambassador, the Marquis de Lafayette (an intimate of the Founding Father, who fought several battles alongside the Americans), to welcome Rochambeau, and the Newport citizenry realized that the French had come not to take things for themselves but to assist the colonists.

Then there was Rochambeau himself: He was imposing, masculine, cordial, and without pretense. The general quickly won the Americans' respect, and the town of Newport began planning celebrations in his honor.

Rochambeau—his full name was Jean-Baptiste Donatien de Vimeur, comte de Rochambeau—was a nobleman. In 1780 he was appointed lieutenant general by Louis XVI and given command of the entire French army in America. He had been ordered to regard Washington as his superior, and it was a testament to his humility and professionalism that he agreed to that subservient role.

Rochambeau enjoyed plush headquarters at the Vernon House on Clarke Street in Newport, which still stands. It was originally the home of William Vernon, a merchant who abandoned his residence during the British occupation. On March 6, 1781, nine months after Rochambeau arrived in Newport, Washington met with the French general there. It would be one of several meetings to plan an assault on Yorktown. The code name for the plan was Expédition Particulière (the Special Expedition). By this time, the French soldiers, who had been quartered during the winter at various Newport homes, were rested and ready to aid the American cause.

The two generals had subsequent meetings (including one in Wethersfield, Connecticut), and by late summer 1781 it was clear to both that Lord Cornwallis had established a precarious defensive position in Yorktown. In addition, a French fleet under Admiral DeGrasse was sailing to the Chesapeake Bay from the West Indies. Rochambeau convinced Washington that it was the perfect time to strike. Together they assembled an army of twelve hundred men and marched them, their artillery, and their supplies hundreds of miles to Virginia. They arrived at Williamsburg on September 14, 1781, and two weeks later converged on Yorktown. Rochambeau, because of his experience, oversaw the siege, and on October 19 Cornwallis was forced to surrender.

After the war, Rochambeau returned to France, where he was named governor of Picardy and appointed the commander of Calais and Alsace. During the French Revolution, he was arrested in the Reign of Terror but was able to escape the guillotine, and was later pensioned by Napoleon Bonaparte.

In January 1789 Washington wrote to Rochambeau: "I cannot but hope, that the Independence of America, to which you have so gloriously contributed, will prove a blessing to mankind. It is thus you see, My dear Count, in retirement, upon my farm, I speculate on the fate of nations; amusing myself with innocent Reveries, that mankind will, one day, grow happier and better."

Rochambeau's exploits during the American Revolution are today commemorated in Newport with an impressive, life-size statue. I stopped to see it in the summer of 2019 on my way to Brooklin, Maine, for vacation. The monument, sculpted by Fernand Hamar, was erected in 1934. A high, curved seawall follows the contour of a small plaza. The statue is well situated in King Park overlooking the bay. It sits on a high pedestal and shows Rochambeau with one arm outstretched toward the water. It's one of several replicas, following one erected in Washington, D.C., in 1902, and one in 1933 in Paris on the Avenue Pierre 1er de Serbie.

Over time, the monument in Newport has been damaged by weather, and in 2019 it required $250,000—raised by the Alliance Française of Newport—to restore. A ceremony was held that year at the bay-side park to unveil the completed project.

As the sun was setting, I took another walk around the statue and then sat down to make a sketch of it. I noticed details, such as the long row of buttons on Rochambeau's uniform and a folded map in one of his hands. I thought of Rochambeau's legacy and his waging war three thousand miles away from home. It made me wonder how many tourists actually come to the memorial—and how many appreciate France's role in our fight for independence.

The Americans face overwhelming odds against a brutal regiment at Camden.

Without Mercy

CAMDEN BATTLEFIELD SITE · *Camden, South Carolina*

I N SPRING 2017, my wife, Charlotte, and I spent a long weekend at our friend Stephanie Koven's house in the Deep South. The house—or rather mansion—is known as Mulberry Plantation. It's about three miles from the center of Camden, South Carolina (population: 6,900), and has been in Stephanie's family for generations. Mulberry, built in 1820, is a brick structure shaded by moss-covered live oaks, looking like a set from *Gone With the Wind*. It had originally been the home of the celebrated Civil War diarist Mary Boykin Chestnut, who wrote the classic *Diary from Dixie* (still in print), an important chronicle of everyday life during the Confederacy. We enjoyed walks through a pine forest, had drinks in the library—which has a set of dueling pistols—and ate sumptuous meals, such as quail, grits, and buttered biscuits.

When we returned to Manhattan, Camden lingered, and I grew curious about the locale's history. Upon doing a little research, I discovered, to my surprise, that there's a story quite different from the restful one I'd experienced. If I was ignorant of this chapter on the road to independence, there was a reason. My early schoolbooks had left out most of its details.

The Battle of Camden, which took place on August 6, 1780, was one of the bloodiest of the Revolution. Its principal antagonists were the American general Horatio Gates, victor in 1777

[133

at the Saratoga campaign, and his nemesis, the British colonel Banastre Tarleton. The result was not a flag-waving moment. The Patriots were slaughtered in one of their worst defeats. Moreover, General Gates became a pariah for his cowardly retreat, which almost cost him a court-martial.

To fill in what my textbooks left out, Camden was part of a campaign the British began in February 1780. With England locked in a stalemate with the northern colonists, the Redcoats looked to the South to gain an advantage. Camden was General Cornwallis's most important interior garrison and supply depot. The town was strategically located near navigable rivers and Indian trails and was about a hundred miles from the major port of Charleston. As the British built up their fortifications, Congress and General Washington grew increasingly alarmed. Measures were needed to counter the offensive.

On July 25, 1780, General Gates joined forces with General de Kalb's Patriot camp at Deep River, North Carolina. The next day, Gates took full command of both troops and set out for Camden, about 120 miles away. Against advice from his officers, he chose a direct route that took the men through swampy, pretty much impenetrable terrain. If he'd taken a less direct pathway, he'd have been able to collect much-needed food and supplies in a more Patriot-friendly area.

A week and a half later, on August 7, Gates received support from two thousand North Carolina militia at Rugeley's Mill, fifteen miles north of Camden, under the command of Colonel James Calwell. This doubled the army's size to forty-one hundred. In a few days, Gates gained further reinforcement from seven hundred Virginia militiamen. He became overconfident, however, and failed to recognize a growing obstacle: more than half of his men were incapacitated. A sudden epidemic of dysentery, brought on by rations of molasses mixed with unripe apples, had rendered them listless and weary. Nevertheless, Gates stubbornly pushed on, and suffered the consequences.

When the rebel and Redcoat armies met, on August 16, more than two thousand British, with the aid of some Loyalist regiments, defeated the much larger—though depleted—American force. What followed was brutal. As the rebels retreated, many of them in a panic, Colonel Tarleton relentlessly pursued them, killing soldiers even as they knelt in surrender. Survivors ran, leaving behind their guns and horses.

Gates, the rebel commander, abandoned his army and fled on horseback; he rode for several days, until he reached Hillsborough, North Carolina, almost two hundred miles away. Though some have argued that Gates tried repeatedly to rally his men, most historians agree that the general had failed them.

"Was there ever so precipituous a flight?" Alexander Hamilton wrote mockingly to James Duane, a stateman from New York, on September 6, 1780. "A hundred and eighty miles in three days and a half. It does admirable credit to the activity of any at his time of life." Gates would never again be chosen for high command.

Camden was a serious setback for the Continental Army, but as the war continued to rage farther south, the British gradually weakened. They suffered defeats at Kings Mountain, North Carolina, on October 7, 1780, and at Cowpens, South Carolina, on January 17, 1781. The regulars would eventually be victorious at Guilford Courthouse, North Carolina, on March 15, but it was a costly triumph, with 550 men dead or wounded. The end grew closer, though, with Yorktown the final blow.

Today, you may visit the 476-acre core battlefield at Camden, located off US Highway 521 on Flat Rock Road. It's bordered at one end by Gum Swamp Creek and is roughly three miles long.

There are several walking trails with historical markers, and a podcast at the visitor center describes the battle in great detail.

You may not get a chance to hold dueling pistols or sample quail and grits, but you'll discover a beautiful part of the United States and perhaps reflect on the loss of life incurred during a major Revolutionary War battle.

The Swamp Fox

FRANCIS MARION STATUE · *Marion, South Carolina*
CITY OF CHARLESTON · *South Carolina*

WHEN I used to think of the battles of the Revolution, what came to mind were Bunker Hill, Lexington, Trenton, Saratoga, Yorktown, and maybe Brandywine. It's a short list and almost everything on it is in the Northeast, where I've lived most of my life. I was born in Boston, where the Freedom Trail is a popular tourist attraction and whose schools are closed on Patriots' Day.

But much of the Revolution was fought in the South. In fact, there were almost as many battles waged in the Carolinas as in all of the other colonies. Campaigns took place in Cowpens, Kings Mountain, Camden, Waxhaws, Eutaw Springs, and Charleston. Charleston was one of the most significant. The Seige was a decisive victory for the British (May 12, 1780), giving them a crucial advantage after their earlier triumph at Savannah, Georgia. For the Americans, the loss of Charleston was devastating; fifty-five hundred Continentals were captured, wounded, or killed, and they lost a vast store of weapons and supplies. It was one of the worst defeats of the Revolution.

Washington's officers had been outmaneuvered, but they had not been caught unawares. The general, from his headquarters at Morristown, New Jersey, had predicted that Charleston would be a target, because he knew the British had altered their

strategy. Exasperated by a stalemate in the North, the Redcoats were now on the move in the South, and Washington
needed to prepare his army for an attack. In September 1779,
after the fall of Savannah (December 29, 1778), he ordered Major General Benjamin Lincoln, who had served in the Massachusetts militia, to defend Charleston at all costs. Lincoln,
however, needed more soldiers. Washington, in turn, needed
soldiers around New York City. There were simply not enough
men to go around.

Rarely were there more than twenty thousand soldiers in the
Continental Army. Many deserted—as many as twenty percent—to go back to their farms. Others left because they were
not paid enough or because they preferred enlisting with their
state militias, which required a shorter term of service and did
not demand as much discipline. Still others were wounded or
too ill to continue to fight. Without adequate reinforcements,
Lincoln was forced to surrender to Sir Henry Clinton.

In the ensuing months, the British would keep the pressure
on in the South. By fighting in the lower colonies, they hoped
to gain more support from Loyalists. They overestimated the
number of Loyalists, however—and they also underestimated
the rebels.

Enter Colonel Francis Marion. The "Swamp Fox," as he
was known, was a pivotal figure in the fight against the British
in present-day Florida, Georgia, and the Carolinas. A native
South Carolinian, Marion formed a band of marauders who
used guerrilla tactics to terrorize the British troops as they
marched through the backcountry of what was largely unset-
tled territory. Like Robin Hood, Marion—often using snipers
in trees—would play a deadly game of cat and mouse, emerging on horseback from the shadows to surprise the Redcoats,
who had scant knowledge of the area, and then retreating back

The Georgia swamps and dense forests created a safe hideaway for Marion and his raiders.

to the safety of the deep swamps. Again and again, the British were randomly attacked, and no sooner had they succeeded in thwarting the raiders, they were ambushed again.

According to historian John Oller, who published a biography of Marion in 2016, "Banastre Tarleton [a British general] once embarked on a seven-hour hunt for Marion, trudging through twenty-six miles of miserable swamps and narrow gorges. Marion, in turn, took his men on a thirty-five-mile jaunt, down along a river and then across another, through several bogs, always staying beyond shouting distance of his pursuers. Tarleton reported to Cornwallis, that because of Marion's head start and 'the difficulties of the country,' he was unable to track him down: 'Come my boys! Let us go back, and we will soon find the Gamecock [Thomas Sumter]. But as for this damned old fox, the Devil himself could not catch him!'"

And that's how Francis Marion became the Swamp Fox.

Over time, Marion and the rest of the American forces in the South, commanded by Nathanael Greene, would sufficiently wear down the British that they lost their resolve. Although the Redcoats were winning the majority of the battles, for example, at Waxhaws, their casualties continued to mount and the Patriots were not giving in. Parliament also began to question whether the regulars could prevail. Cornwallis's fall at Yorktown, in Virginia, where he was forced to surrender eight thousand men, proved England's worst fears, and the war was at its final turning point.

Over the ensuing decades, Marion would become a folk hero. Throughout the 1800s, many American towns and counties were named after him. Even into the twentieth century, Marion had enough name recognition that Walt Disney produced a TV series (1959), starring Leslie Nielsen as Marion, based on his exploits. Also, the 2000 movie *The Patriot*, starring

Mel Gibson, is based partially on the Swamp Fox. There's even a tasty stew associated with him. Recently I met Ann Close, a literary editor for many years at Knopf, through the artist Ed Sorel. She and I were talking about her years growing up in the South and she mentioned Pine Bark Stew, which she remembers eating in Georgia, where Marion was a revered figure. "It was easy to make and was supposedly prepared in the woody swamps where Marion's men often camped," she told me. "It's a spicy fish concoction and was probably named after the pine bark used to cook the fires under it. Another theory is that the root from pine trees was used to season the dish. In any case, it was a fond memory of my childhood and shows that Marion's legacy was still intact."

There's a statue in Marion, South Carolina, of the Swamp Fox —the first ever made of him—in front of the Marion County Courthouse. The sculptor Ramojus Mozoliauskas created the larger-than-life-size likeness. State Senator Ralph Gasque presided over its dedication on April 9, 1976, and Robert D. Bass, a distinguished Marion scholar and the author of *The Swamp Fox*, gave the address. The inscription on the pedestal reads:

FRANCIS MARION; BORN AT ST. JOHN'S PARISH, 1732; DIED FEBRUARY 27, 1795, BURIED IN BELLE ISLE PLANTATION, BERKELEY COUNTY, SC; 1759, FRENCH AND INDIAN WAR; 1761, CHEROKEE UPRISING; 1775, CAPTAIN 2ND SC REGIMENT; 1775, COMMANDER FORT DORCHESTER; 1776, MAJOR, BATTLE OF SULLIVAN'S ISLAND; 1777, LT. COLONEL 2ND SC REGIMENT; 1780, BRIGADIER GENERAL MILITIA.

But perhaps an even greater opportunity to learn about Marion is to visit the city of Charleston, where he fought many of his battles. It was there that he led his company to capture Fort

Motte from the British, and it was there, in the following year, that he thwarted the English before they could take the city.

The buildings of Charleston themselves are worth seeing. It's a virtual gallery of some of America's greatest antebellum architecture. The entire Charleston Historic District is a national landmark, and Charleston is home to an array of building styles—Colonial, Georgian, Regency, Federal, Adamesque, Classical Revival, Greek Revival, and Queen Anne.

Most of the grand structures were built after Marion's time, however: The Carolinas of the 1700s, with the exception of a few cities, were far less developed than the northern colonies. To a large extent, they were what amounted to territories, with more wilderness than habitable land.

For Marion, though, that was a distinct advantage in his fight against the Redcoats. They never saw him coming.

Planter Patriot

GEORGE WASHINGTON'S GARDENS
Mount Vernon, Virginia

OR AN aspiring gentleman in colonial America, few things mattered more than status. A gentleman was judged by his manners, his clothes, his words, even his handwriting—and George Washington was no exception. The future president paid very close attention to his deportment, and, perhaps most of all, how he dressed. He went as far as to custom-design a blue band for his uniform to set him apart from his officers. From a young age, Washington studied *The Rules of Civility and Decent Behavior*, a popular manual of the time, whose maxims had roots in France during the 1500s. He copied the rules repeatedly by hand so he could memorize them. Today, some are awkwardly phrased; others still make sense. Among the 110 rules:

In the Presence of Others Sing not to yourself with a humming Noise, nor Drum with your Fingers or Feet . . . Do not Puff up the Cheeks, Loll not out the tongue[,] rub the Hands, or beard, thrust out the lips, or bite them or keep the Lips too open or too Closed . . .

"Appearances were everything," the historian David Mc-Cullough once told me. "For Washington it started with his house. He was very particular about each aspect of Mount Vernon. He chose the wallpaper and furnishings that would impress others and elevate his social standing." McCullough, who won a Pulitzer Prize for his book *1776*, added: "And it was his array of gardens and crops, I believe, that he prized the most. He wanted to be perceived as a Virginia planter more so, even, than being president."

Other Founding Fathers—Madison, Monroe, and Jefferson, for example—also prided themselves on being planters. Like them, Washington supervised his own gardens' planning, organization, and cultivation. It was not unusual for the commander in chief, hoe in hand, to be seen sowing seeds for his lettuce and onions (although, it must be noted, almost all the work was done by slaves).

There are several distinct gardens at Mount Vernon: an ornamental garden, a vegetable garden, a botanical garden, and a vineyard.

The ornamental, or upper garden as it was more often called, is a formal layout that displays Washington's expertise in horticultural design, and he enjoyed showing it off to his guests. It has a formal geometry and creates a different layout to the looser configuration of the adjacent bowling green. The garden had several planting beds divided by crushed pebble pathways. Each bed was bordered with dwarf boxwoods, one of which was trimmed to form a fleur-de-lis. According to the current experts working at Mount Vernon, this may have been a nod to the French alliance.

In the upper garden, an impressive brick greenhouse contained tropical plants. In addition to providing oranges and limes for Mrs. Washington's pantry stores, the greenhouse showcased rare plants from around the world, including an aloe vera from as far away as North Africa.

Located just back of the spinning house, the botanical garden—which Washington referred to as his "little garden"—was of particular interest to the general. It brought out the scientist

Washington prized his vast estate on the Potomac.

in him. It was in a sense his laboratory, where he experimented with new plant varieties and how best to grow them. Foreign diplomats and friends often supplied him with samplings of different seeds from a number of locations. The historian Helen Miller in her 1936 biography of George Mason (a fellow Virginian who was also a planter), noted that Mason sent Washington various cuttings from a number of flowers, including Persian jasmine, and the Guelder Rose.

In April 1786, Washington wrote: "Took the covering off the Plants in my Botanical Garden, and found none living of all those planted the 13th of June last except some of the Acasee or Acacia, flower fence and privy [privet] . . . Whether these plants are unfit for this climate, or whether covering and thereby hiding them entirely from the Sun the whole winter occasioned them to rot, I know not."

As a man of the Enlightenment, Washington based his agricultural knowledge on extensive reading and scientific research, especially of the English experts, and amassed a sizable library on advanced husbandry. His equipment included a thermometer and a weather vane—an exact replica ("the dove of peace") of which still "flies" over Mount Vernon's cupola.

Washington, in addition to knowing about gardening, was well versed in architecture. Mostly self-taught, he knew the rudiments of classical design and was likely familiar with the pattern books of the time, such as Palladio's treatises on villas and the ancient orders. Mount Vernon is a perfect synthesis of many of his ideas. Over time he transformed it from a modest farmhouse, which he had inherited from his half brother Lawrence (who died at thirty-four), into a stately manor. New wings, a colonnade, and several outbuildings were added, each to match the style of the main house. Washington sought an ideal: a lyrical order within a random, untamed landscape.

Mount Vernon became Washington's personal paradise. Numerous paintings depict him on the grounds of his Potomac plantation, enjoying gatherings with friends, family, and dignitaries, such as Lafayette, who came more than once to visit. Men and women of Virginia's high society were frequent guests. Other paintings, however, show Washington with his slaves. In one canvas, by Julius Stearns, *Washington as Farmer at Mount Vernon* (1853), the general is looking on as they toil in the fields. The painting is a distorted depiction of slavery as a merry existence, with well-groomed Black men and women harvesting golden wheat in the hot sun. This view was not unusual for the 1850s, and much later, as well.

Washington may have been a compassionate man in certain respects, but he was not, for the most part, when it came to his slaves. Sometimes he made them work from dawn to dusk, even into their eighties. Most of them lived in tiny quarters, sometimes six to a room. Punishments were doled out for small infractions. Mount Vernon may have been a paradise to Washington, but it was anything but to his enslaved workers.

Today tour guides address the subject and will answer your questions. And on Mount Vernon's website, you'll find informative essays and videos that shed light on what the African Americans endured. There are profiles, too, of individual slaves, such as Ona Judge, Caesar, Christopher Sheels, and Caroline Branham.

"It is but the home of a Patriot."

A Family Legacy

PEACEFIELD (JOHN ADAMS HOUSE)
Quincy, Massachusetts

HE BOSTON Massacre, 1774, is remembered for the killing of American civilians by British soldiers, but what of the lawyer who defended those soldiers at trial? It was, of all people, one of the Founding Fathers: John Adams, a man who believed in equal justice, however unpopular. And he won the case.

Adams was neither wealthy nor dashing; he was relatively short, balding, and unprepossessing. He had, however, a brilliant mind. For the HBO series *John Adams* (2008), producer Tom Hanks cast Paul Giamatti in the lead role. The choice was met with the approval of the historian David McCullough, who wrote the book on which the series was based. "Adams was not exactly movie-star handsome," McCullough has said to me, "nor were his times glamorous. I made it clear to Hanks that I did not want a costume pageant. People's clothes were often dirty, their hair was stringy, their boots were muddy. It was a time of hardship and disease. Adams built his own stone walls at his house, cut his own hay. He and his wife, Abigail, could have afforded slaves but made a conscious decision not to own them."

For years McCullough has worked to promote Adams's legacy, not only with his bestselling books but also with a campaign to create a monument to the Founding Father in Washington, D.C. Unfortunately, it has not enjoyed much success. Once at a fundraiser for the Adams memorial I got a chance to ask him why this project has been so difficult to get off the ground. He said he guessed that "Adams was never very well liked, even in his own time. He was stubborn and argumentative. That reputation," he said, "however unfair, lingers today."

In spite of his critics, Adams achieved much success: he was ambassador, vice president, and president. There may not yet be a memorial to him in D.C., but his house in Quincy, Massachusetts, which he lived in with his wife, Abigail, is now a National Historic Site. It's a quaint but distinguished clapboard house, with several dormers and a gambrel roof. It was once on an estate of some three hundred acres which the Adams' named Peacefield. A sign outside the house, added more recently, is printed with a quote from Adams: "It is but the home of a Patriot."

The property is now much smaller, a bit less than fifteen acres. Quincy (the town was part of Braintree during Adams's time) has changed considerably over the years, and is far more developed. John Adams's great-great-granddaughter Abigail Adams Homans remembered it from her childhood at the close of the nineteenth century. She wrote in *Education by Uncles* (1966), her memoir: "The Quincy that I knew in my childhood now lives in memory—a quiet country town, with little relation to the present, bustling suburban city. The family house on Adams Street has survived almost intact, complete with some of the family pictures, most of the china and all of the furniture, a curious jumble of federal and diplomatic debris."

The original owners of the house were members of the Leonard Vassall family, Loyalists who fled to England during the Revolution. John and Abigail purchased the house in 1787 while they were abroad during Adams's tenure as American minister to Britain (1785-1788). They had outgrown their small farmhouse, a Saltbox on nearby Penn's Hill, where they had lived since 1764 and where their children, among them John Quincy, were born.

Their new home was bigger but still needed enlarging, at least according to Abigail. The story goes that upon seeing the house again after returning from England with her husband, she sat down and wept. The house looked much smaller than she'd remembered it. "In height and breadth, it feels like a wren's house," she wrote in a letter to her daughter on July 7, 1788. "Be sure you wear no feathers, and let Col. Smith come without heels to his shoes, or he will not be able to walk upright."

Her husband was sufficiently moved, and promised Abigail that he would add to the house so she might have a proper room for her French furniture, which they had acquired while Adams was commissioner to France (1777–79). It took some years to complete the alterations, but he made good on his promise.

Years later, their descendants made other changes. At the northwest corner of the property stands the Stone Library, built by Charles Francis Adams (John and Abigail's grandson) to preserve the family books and papers. It was made of solid Quincy granite, and Homans remembers it as "a delicious sanctuary" with a gallery above, which one reached by a shaky little ladder that "was so easily detachable that one could either maroon an enemy up there or else, by bad luck, be marooned oneself."

The letters between Abigail and John would undoubtedly have been part of the library's collection. I asked McCullough about them: "John and Abigail are a great love story," he told me. "The two of them poured out their feelings to one another in their letters. They are candid and honest. There are over a thousand that survive and they're a lens into what life was like then, not only for them, but for the country, too."

The letters start with their courtship in 1762 and continue throughout the years of John's political career. They contain his thoughts about the Continental Congress and his diplomatic insights about Europe, among other topics. And they contain Abigail's reflections on the struggle for independence, the role of women in society, and the daily activities of overseeing Peacefield.

It's a remarkable record and it's fortunate so many of the letters were saved. In contrast, in accordance with the custom of the day, Jefferson destroyed his wife's letters and Martha Washington destroyed all but two of her husband's.

On March 31, 1776, Abigail writes: "I long to hear that you have declared an independency. And, by the way, in the new code of laws which I suppose it will be necessary for you to make, I desire you would remember the ladies and be more generous and favorable to them than your ancestors. Do not put such unlimited power into the hands of the husbands. Remember, all men would be tyrants if they could."

In a letter from July 1776, John expresses his thoughts following the signing of the Declaration: "I am apt to believe that it will be celebrated, by succeeding Generations, as the great anniversary Festival. It ought to be commemorated, as the Day of Deliverance by solemn Acts of Devotion to God Almighty. It ought to be solemnized with Pomp and Parade, with Shews, Games, Sports, Guns, Bells, Bonfires and Illuminations from one End of this Continent to the other."

Peacefield is often mentioned in the correspondence. The couple remained there till they died. Today the house is accessible to the public and is open throughout the year. It is humble compared with Mount Vernon. But it befits the man who lived

there. As Adams once wrote of himself: "It has been fashion-
able to call me The Venerable. Don't call me Godlike Adams,
The Father of His Country, The Founder of his Republic, or
The Founder of the American Empire. These titles belong to no
man, but to the American people in general."

A young British officer makes a pact with the devil
(after a self-portrait sketch by Major John André).

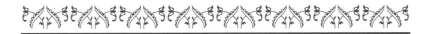

Soldier Spy

MAJOR JOHN ANDRÉ MONUMENT · *Tappan, New York*
YALE ART GALLERY · *New Haven, Connecticut*

ROGER ANGELL, a longtime editor and writer at *The New Yorker*, is a man of many stories. Over the years, at our weekly lunches, I've been all ears. Whether it's playing Ping-Pong with James Thurber, visiting Somerset Maugham on the Riviera, or serving in the Pacific, Roger never disappoints—even on the verge of his hundred and first birthday.

"Adam," he asked me one day, which discussing my book project over barley soup and tarragon chicken salad, "have you ever been to Tappan, New York?"

"No," I said. "Should I go?"

"Yes. It's where Major André was hanged."

"Major André?" I asked.

"It's quite a tale," he said. "Do you want to hear it?"

I nodded.

"André conspired with Benedict Arnold and was caught in Tappan [in 1780]. Washington had put Arnold in charge of the fort at West Point. But Arnold had already planned to switch sides, and he got André to smuggle plans of the fort. Arnold got twenty thousand pounds from the Brits for the plans. The Americans hated him after that; and later, the English hated him too. André, on the other hand, is remembered as a martyr."

"How was he caught?"

"Three militiamen found him walking on a back road. They were suspicious and told him to remove some of his civilian clothes. Then they found the plans in his boots. Soon afterward, one of them got hold of Washington, who was headquartered in the area. There was a trial in the local meetinghouse and André was found guilty."

Roger went on.

"One summer, many years ago," Roger said, adjusting his cap from the Maine Wooden Boat School, "I was staying at a house in the town of Palisades and an old gardener named Post—I forgot his first name—came up to me. 'Do you wanna see something int'resting?' 'Sure,' I said. Post pulled out an old leather pouch wrapped with string. He opened it carefully, peeling back layers of thin hide. Inside were pieces of what looked like small, grimy twigs. 'What's *that?*' I asked.

'It's Major Andre's toe bone!'

I asked him how he got the strange-looking thing. He was holding it like it was a relic of Joan of Arc. 'One of my ancestors was the gravedigger who buried André after he was hanged. He dug up this bone later and we've kept it in the family all these years.'"

Roger's tale piqued my interest in the notorious spy. I told him I was puzzled about why an American like Post would covet remains of an enemy officer.

"André was a charismatic figure in his time," Roger explained. "He was dashing and a bigwig in London society. He wrote poetry and maybe even wrote some plays, I think. Look him up."

And look him up I did. My research led me down several

rabbit holes, one deeper than the next. I learned from a book by Benson Lossing, *A Pictorial Field Guide to the American Revolution*, that André, among his many other talents, was a gifted artist. On the day before his execution he drew a pen-and-ink sketch of himself sitting at a desk, looking very dapper. I wondered how he had the stomach to finish it. I learned later that the picture is in the collection of the art museum at Yale, where I teach, so I made an appointment to see it. Holding the drawing in my hand, I marveled at the delicate skill of André's pen strokes. They were steady and confident, not what you'd expect of someone heading to the gallows.

To the British, he would become a national hero. Forty years after his death, George III (yes, he was still king) requested that André's remains be transferred to England for burial in Westminster Abbey. When his body was exhumed, tree roots were found wrapped around the coffin. They were removed and replanted in England. If André had reached an ignominious end, at least he was now being granted immortality in the halls of one of Europe's greatest cathedrals.

On a recent trip to London I visited Westminster. André's tomb was in the nave, set among monuments of such figures as Mary Queen of Scots, Richard III, Winston Churchill, Charles Dickens, and George Bernard Shaw. The tomb shows a mourning figure of Britannia with a lion on the top of a sarcophagus. On the front is a relief depicting George Washington in a tent receiving a petition (in which André asked for a soldier's death by firing squad) and a flag of truce. Major André is being led away to be hanged.

As I stooped to see the details more closely, I wondered if the punishment fit the crime. Washington certainly thought so. (After all, the American spy Nathan Hale had been hanged from a tree by the British in 1776.) When André arrived at his execution, he apparently applied the noose to himself and said, "Let it be known that I died a brave man. This will be but a momentary pang."

In 2019, closer to my home in New York, I followed through on Roger's suggestion and made a visit to Tappan. It's is a small town in Rockland County, overlooking the Hudson River, with a tiny main street of small shops and eateries. My first stop was the old tavern called the '76 House. It is the same building in which André was jailed for a few days before his execution. I found a table in the main dining room and ordered the onion soup. My waitress, Lara, was pleased to answer my questions about the local tourist attraction.

"Yeah, André is a big deal here, at least to history types," she said. "I remember as a kid that my middle school teacher took our class here to see where he was jailed. It was a teeny room, about the size of a phone booth. I don't think it even had a stool." She pointed. "It was right over there by the door."

I looked but all I saw was a small waiter station with oil and vinegar, napkins, and some salt and pepper shakers.

"The previous owner tore it down because he wanted room for more tables," Lara said. "He got fined by the town for destroying a historical marker. If you're really interested, you can visit the memorial where he died, just up the hill about half a mile."

I paid my bill, left the restaurant, and drove up to the monument. There, on a cul-de-sac of suburban homes, was a granite block, about two feet high and set in a tiny circle of lawn surrounded by an iron gate. Within the stone is inlaid a bronze plaque, dating from 1879 (and originally subsidized by the millionaire Cyrus Field), with a lengthy description of André's demise. About twenty feet away there was a basketball net, and several teenagers were practicing their jump shot. They were bouncing the ball on the pavement and the sound ricocheted down the block. *Whump-whump-whump.*

Quite a contrast to the halls of Westminster Abbey.

This leafy haven in Connecticut is where two generals plotted their grand finale.

Meeting of Minds

WEBB DEAN STEVENS MUSEUM
Wethersfield, Connecticut

HARTFORD, CONNECTICUT, has a rich history. It was founded in 1635 by English colonists led by the Reverend Thomas Hooker, and was later the home of the American abolitionist Harriet Beecher Stowe (1811–1896) and of Mark Twain (1835–1910). For much of the twentieth century, the city was the cradle of the insurance industry. In recent times, however, Hartford, like many other American cities, has suffered the effects of urban decay: overdevelopment, deindustrialization, and abandoned infrastructure.

But just a few miles to the south, in the shadow of this metropolis, there is another world, one untouched by city sprawl. The picturesque river town of Old Wethersfield, with its row of preserved eighteenth-century homes and redbrick churches, looks like a New England version of Colonial Williamsburg. Picket fences and manicured lawns impart a bucolic air to this historic corner of the state.

During the Revolution, Wethersfield's population consisted largely of merchants in international trade and farmers. Among the crops were wheat, barley, and red onions—the town's greatest export. In fact, there were so many onions that their aroma could be smelled for miles. John Adams visited the town in 1771 and recorded his impressions in his diary: "I have just spent the morning riding through paradise . . . we went up the steeple of the Wethersfield meeting-house, from whence is the most grand and beautiful prospect in the world, at least that I ever saw."

At 211 Main Street, not far from where Adams stood (the meetinghouse is now the First Church of Christ), sits one of the town's finest period homes: the Joseph Webb House. It's here in this clapboard dwelling along the Connecticut River a crucial event took place in the struggle for independence. George Washington, as was the case so often, was at the center of it. He stayed here for a period in May 1781 to plan a strategic offensive against the British—one he hoped would end the war, then in its sixth year. In the months leading up to that spring, the Continental Army had suffered a string of defeats in North Carolina, including one at Guilford Courthouse (March 15), the last of which was under the command of one of Washington's most able field generals, Nathanael Greene.

Washington had arranged for a conference at the Webb House with the general Comte de Rochambeau, who had crossed the Atlantic to aid the American cause and had been stationed in Newport, Rhode Island, for several months prior. Wethersfield was a logical location, as it was roughly halfway between Newport and New Windsor, New York, where Washington and his army were encamped. Each general arrived for the conference with an entourage of about thirty men, most of whom were quartered in other homes in Wethersfield. One of Washington's accompanying officers was Henry Knox, who was in charge of artillery during 1776's Siege of Boston.

Over the next five days Washington and Rochambeau were involved in intense, often heated discussions about whether to either attack Yorktown, Virginia—where the British were garrisoned—or New York City, which the British had occupied since the start of the war. These discussions had begun in Newport in March 1781. Washington still felt the stinging loss of New York as a thorn in his side, ever since 1776, when the British won the Battle of Brooklyn. He believed now was the time to strike the City, because many of the Redcoats in New York, under General Clinton, had headed south to fight in the Carolinas.

Initially, Rochambeau, who did not speak English and wrote his notes on a piece of paper that were then translated, sided with Washington, if for no other reason than to be diplomatic. In truth, though, he believed that his French forces, combined with Washington's—a total of eighty-three hundred—were still not sufficient to challenge Clinton's army. Furthermore, the French ships, under Rochambeau's overall command, had larger hulls than those of the British and were more likely to stall in the shallow waters surrounding Manhattan. Eventually, the Frenchman got his way and he and Washington resolved to attack Yorktown. That battle spelled the last big defeat for the British, and the war for independence would soon be over.

Today the Webb House is a landmark on the National Register, and is managed by a dedicated board with a sizable endowment. Ann Burton, a member of that board, is a distinguished scholar of American and British history and has spent some twenty years connected with the house. There are few people with more knowledge about the Webb home (part of the Webb-Stevens-Deane Museum) than she has.

"It's important to realize," Ann told me over the phone in 2020, "that Washington and Rochambeau met here because Wethersfield, and the Webb House in particular, was a real destination. The house was known to the locals as Hospitality House because of all the social events that took place there." The Webbs were a prominent family who had made a fortune

IN THE FOUNDERS' FOOTSTEPS

in trade. Many dignitaries paid calls there (as well as at the neighboring homes of Silas Deane, a delegate to the Continental Congress, and Isaac Stevens, a successful trader). "It's not surprising that Washington chose this peaceful, welcoming setting," she said. "It was almost like going to Camp David for today's politicians."

I asked Anne what made Wethersfield such an idyllic spot.

"The river was very much part of the life of this town," she said. "Sailing vessels would glide by at all times of the day. We recently discovered a needlework sampler from our research, made by a young girl from an eighteenth-century female academy nearby, which shows how beautiful this place looked among the river and trees."

Anne studied at Oxford, has taught at Brooklyn College, and has also been an associate dean of the Faculty of Arts and Sciences at New York University. She was eager to tell me about an archaeological dig recently completed on the Webb site. "We discovered some extraordinary things," she said. "There were coins found with the image of Charles the First, so we know there was another settlement here many years before. We also found musket balls from the 1700s that were French, which confirms that French officers were here with Washington."

What had prompted the dig?

Anne explained that the museum had decided to make a new addition to its compound, and it was required by the state to examine the site first for any historical artifacts and information. "Perhaps our most interesting find," she said, "was a palisade, or defensive wall, that was built to protect the people of Wethersfield from the Pequot Indians. It confirms that the Indians were here long before we came. They recognized the natural wonder of this location hundreds, if not thousands, of years before the Europeans."

The Webb House is owned by the National Society of Colonial Dames. From as early as 1916, the house has been me-
ticulously maintained as a historical structure. Wallace Nutting,
an antiquarian, photographer, and author, bought the house in
February of that year and set about making it look as authentic
as possible. During World War I he was forced to sell it to the
Dames.

These days the house is a living museum, and it holds numerous events. On Memorial Day, there's a Revolutionary
War reenactment, where visitors can see the Fifth Connecticut Regiment in colonial uniform, listen to colonial music, and
watch demonstrations of musket firing and open-fire cooking.
During Christmas, decorations installed throughout the house
show visitors how the holiday season has evolved over the last
three centuries.

If Washington and Rochambeau could return to Wethersfield, I think they'd be quite comfortable here. Little of this
picturesque town has changed.

Poplar Forest was a handsome retreat for a Founding Father in his final days.

A Secret Setting

POPLAR FOREST · *Forest, Virginia*

PAUL REVERE, whose midnight ride saved the Founding Father John Hancock from certain capture and probable imprisonment, is not the only hero who rescued a pillar of the Revolution. In 1781, six years after Revere's claim to fame, another hero—John "Jack" Jouett—saved the life of Thomas Jefferson.

On June 3, 1781, five years into the war, British forces led by Lord Cornwallis, Banastre Tarleton, and the newly turned traitor Benedict Arnold were conducting raids through Virginia along the James River. They were closing in on members of the Virginia Assembly, and Jefferson, then governor of the colony, was in their sights. Tarleton, or "the Butcher," as he was known, was dispatched to capture Jefferson at his estate in Charlottesville. If not for the local militia captain Jack Jouett, Tarleton might well have succeeded—and the rest, as they say, would be history. But the day before Tarleton could reach the estate, the twenty-six-year-old Jouett spied him camping with his men and knew they planned to attack Monticello.

Jouett sped on horseback forty miles to Jefferson's home to alert the governor. According to Jefferson's account from one of his Memorandum Books, Jouett knew the "by-ways of the neighborhood, passed the enemy's encampment, rode all night, and before sun-rise of [June 4] called at Monticello." Legend has it that Jefferson offered Jouett a glass of Madeira before the young man rode off to warn the other assemblymen.

Jefferson made plans for a getaway for his wife and children. He ordered a carriage to take them to safety at a nearby farm. As for himself, he hesitated before abandoning his vast property. According to Christopher Hudson, a neighbor, he remained "perfectly tranquil, and undisturbed," even as Tarleton's men were ascending the mountain toward him. It was classic Jefferson, cool and deliberate. What was he waiting for? Did he want to collect some of his papers? His scientific instruments? Or read one last chapter of Locke?

We will never know. But when he finally put his house in order, he set out to join his family. Jefferson narrowly escaped: He rode his horse through a little-known path in the woods—at one point hiding in the hollow of a tree—just before Tarleton and his soldiers arrived at the front door of Monticello. Jefferson's slaves were inside (some of them had been told to hide their master's valuables underneath the house), and despite being threatened at gunpoint, they refused to reveal his whereabouts.

Tarleton had been outwitted. Turning around abruptly, the English officer made a hasty retreat from Charlottesville. And although he succeeded in rounding up seven legislators as prisoners, most of the assemblymen had escaped to the town of Staunton.

Without Tarleton's band at his heels, Jefferson could plot his family's next move. He decided against returning to Monticello and chose instead to go to Poplar Forest, another estate he owned. It was a secret retreat in Lynchburg, at the foot of the Blue Ridge Mountains, which he had inherited from his father-in-law. He spent the rest of the summer there with his family on its five thousand acres. He had dreamt one day of building a house there, but for now they would live in the over-seer's cottage.

Some would later accuse Jefferson, who had abandoned his post as governor, of cowardice. It would take a hearing before the Virginia Assembly sometime later to defend his honor, and it would stain his reputation for the rest of his life.

Despite these harrowing events, Poplar Forest in subsequent years became Jefferson's little Eden. In 1809, he designed a small—at least by his standards—Palladian villa, set among a group of mulberry trees. It would be an octagonal plan dwelling, with tall French windows and a columned portico. The central space would be a perfect cube, measuring twenty feet in all directions. The exterior was of redbrick with white trim. Jefferson took great pride in his creation: "When finished," he wrote, "it will be the best dwelling house in the state next to Monticello."

For Jefferson, the landscape was every bit as important as the house itself. In 2020, Ann Lucas, research director at the Jefferson Foundation, spoke to me on this point. "Jefferson in-corporated nature in a way that was unique," she said. "Instead of adding brick-and-mortar wings to the main house to create the perfect symmetry for his overall plan, he incorporated al-lées of trees to mimic that geometry. It was a pastoral idea that was very American."

Lucas, who studied architectural history at the University of Virginia which Jefferson also designed—sees a different man at Poplar Forest. "I think Jefferson was more free-spirited in his scheme for Poplar than at Monticello," she said. "He was having fun. He even designed furniture for the house, like Frank Lloyd Wright did in his designs. Maybe Jefferson felt he could try dif-ferent things because he was less restricted and because Poplar was more private than public. He drew inspiration from the natural surroundings and had a fascination with a rock forma-

IN THE FOUNDERS' FOOTSTEPS

tion called the Natural Bridge, which was a few miles from his house. He took excursions there, wrote about it, and invited artists to paint it."

Even while he was president, Jefferson detailed in his letters the construction of Poplar Forest: how the fireplace should be built, the location of the moldings, and how the floorboards needed to be installed. In 1806, he traveled from Washington to supervise the laying of the foundation.

"There are some dramatic double cubes in the bedrooms that look very postmodern," Ann told me. "And the overall plan is a pure octagon, not an elongated one like Monticello. Jefferson was definitely channeling Palladio's Villa Rotonda, which is the same on all four sides."

When the project was complete, Jefferson relished the peace and quiet of his second home. It was sparsely furnished and simply decorated, without wallpaper or highboys. In that sense it was the antithesis of Monticello, and presented a humbler side to Jefferson, more farmer than statesman.

Eventually, Jefferson made a point of regularly visiting Poplar four times a year. If he could have gone more often, he would have. The distractions and responsibilities of Monticello had become a burden. It was not unusual, for example, for strangers to wander onto his Charlottesville property and peer at him through his windows.

Free from such intrusions, Jefferson at Poplar Forest enjoyed the company of his grandchildren, read his books, and inspected his grounds. And wrote. In 1785 he composed *Notes on the State of Virginia*, which contained his ideas on freedom of religion, constitutional government, checks and balances, and individual liberty. There were also passages on the natural resources of Virginia, and even detailed references to the life of the honey bee.

Jefferson also wrote extensively about slavery in *Notes*. And its contents reveal a side to the Founding Father that is disturb-ing. Jefferson's book offered justification of white supremacy and a voiced a belief that whites and Blacks could not live to-gether in a free society. Some of the author's reflections on race are chilling, even in the context of the time.

Jefferson made his last trip to Poplar Forest in 1823, when he settled his grandson Francis Eppes on the property. Ill health prevented further visits, and two years after Jefferson's death, in 1828, Eppes sold Poplar Forest to a neighbor. It remained in private hands until 1982, when a nonprofit corporation bought it. Today, efforts have been made to halt development near the site, and although a golf course adjoins the property, the organi-zation has managed to maintain the feel of Poplar's historic set-ting, even as the property has dwindled to only a hundred acres.

I'm sure it would have saddened Jefferson that Poplar Forest remained in his family for only a short period after his death. It was a world apart from Monticello, but there were times when he preferred it. And in 1781, after a near-death experience at the hands of the villainous Tarleton and the British, he found peace of mind.

Cornwallis and his men are cornered on the Chesapeake.

The Crowning Victory

YORKTOWN BATTLEFIELD

COLONIAL HISTORICAL PARK · *Yorktown, Virginia*

I T'S NOT often one gets invited to a dinner with twenty historians to talk about the Revolution. So when my friend Ed Strauss asked me, I was grateful and eager to attend.

"It's called the American Revolution Roundtable," Ed told me as we lunched over salmon fish cakes at the Coffee House Club. "We meet once a month and have a guest speaker. Members talk about books they've read. It's mostly amateur historians, but we've been humming along since 1958."

"Sounds intriguing," I said. "Who's the next speaker?"

"It's Mary Stockwell. She's just written a book about 'Mad' Anthony Wayne, the American general. Come by tomorrow for our October meeting," Ed said.

Wayne was a figure from the Revolution I didn't know much about until recently, other than that he got his name for being a daring fighter.

When I arrived at the meeting on West 44th Street at the General Society of Mechanics building, I took the elevator to the sixth floor and was greeted in the hall by one of the members. He was about forty, slightly bald, and holding a round metallic object that looked like a bowling ball.

Before I could ask him his name, he thrust the thing at me and said, "Here, hold this."

"Whoa! That's heavy!"

"Guess what it is: a ten-pounder or a twelve-pounder?"

"I'm not sure what you—"

"It's a cannonball from Yorktown. It refers to the weight of the ball. I got it on eBay. It's got a certificate of authenticity. They were made in two-pound increments. This one's a ten."

"Wow!" I said.

"I'm Neil. Welcome to the roundtable."

With my free hand, I shook his. Neil is a doorman in Queens who has been coming to these dinners for a while. "I work the night shift, so I can read books on history when it's quiet," he said. I returned the weighty sphere to him and then he started working the room, passing it around.

After schmoozing during the cocktail hour, I got to know more of the members. Each of them had a day job—some as accountants, lawyers, bankers, actors—but they all had a passion for history. I was impressed with how much they knew. Before long I was knee-deep in the Intolerable Acts (punitive laws passed after the Boston Tea Party), the surrender of "Gentleman Johnny" Burgoyne at Saratoga, and the American fortifications at Fort Stanwix (a defense post in Rome, New York).

As we ate dinner, the speaker gave a PowerPoint presentation about Wayne's fearless, sometimes impulsive actions, which served him well on the battlefield, especially at Brandywine, near Philadelphia. To close out the evening, there was a Q&A and some final comments by the chairman Dave Jacobs. I thanked Ed, told him I planned to come again, and headed off to my apartment.

Back home, I kept thinking about the cannonball. There was something about holding the pockmarked piece of iron. Where was it found on the battlefield? Was it fired by the British or the Americans? Did it kill someone?

And what about Yorktown? I hadn't thought much about the battle (or siege, as it is better known) since my AP World History class with Ms. Schurfranz. I was curious, though, and searched through books I hadn't touched in years. Sandwiched between Henry Steele Commager's *The American Revolution* and James Flexner's *Washington*, I spied a thin volume, published in 1932, which caught my eye: It had a dark blue cover with embossed lettering and an exceptionally dry title: *The Yorktown Book, 1781–1931: The Official Chronicle and Tribute Book*. It was the kind of thing you buy at a flea market for a dollar and never open again.

The book was illustrated with black-and-white photographs and gave a detailed account of the sesquicentennial celebration of the Yorktown campaign, one that lasted for three weeks during fall 1781. Turning the fragile pages, I learned that the commemoration had been a major—and very sizable—event, a kind of Super Bowl for history buffs. More than a hundred thousand people attended. One image showed a large dais set outdoors with various dignitaries: Herbert Hoover, president of the United States at the time; the then-governors of the states that had been the original thirteen colonies; and some direct ancestors of General Rochambeau and Admiral de Grasse, who led the French forces. The celebration lasted three days and was highlighted by the arrival in the Chesapeake of the French navy ships the *Duquesne* and the *Suffren* and the American frigate *Constitution* ("Old Ironsides").

There was good reason for this elaborate anniversary. Yorktown was the coup de grâce, the final great victory of the Revolution. As Hoover said, "This is one of the very few decisive battles in the history of the world."

Though the war dragged on with skirmishes and peace negotiations for almost two more years, until September 3, 1783,

Yorktown was, in effect, the end. But without some luck, the outcome might have been reversed.

In the days leading up to the fight, Washington had resisted attacking Yorktown. His earlier plan, which had preoccupied him for months, was to win back New York from the British, who had occupied the City since 1776. Now, some five years later, General Rochambeau, the leader of the French allied force, was adamant that New York couldn't be won and that Yorktown *could*. The two leaders struggled to find a compromise. Then came unexpected—and very welcome news—that a French fleet of twenty-eight warships, under de Grasse, was on its way to the Chesapeake. Washington seized the moment and, agreed to Rochambeau's plan, and both of them mobilized their armies for a march to Virginia.

Washington's willingness to swallow his pride and change course was crucial to winning the war.

The Siege of Yorktown ended on October 19, 1781, when Cornwallis surrendered. His great mistake was that he had set his own trap, albeit inadvertently. He had staked a position that included ten thousand men, a fort, and a fleet of twelve ships; but with his back to the York River, he was vulnerable. When de Grasse anchored in the Chesapeake, the British were effectively bottlenecked. Cornwallis had assumed that his superior officer, General Clinton, sailing from New York, would provide support. But Clinton came too late—arriving only after Cornwallis signed the capitulation. Cornwallis had earlier pleaded to Clinton in a letter: "We cannot hope to make a long resistance." After six days of steady bombardment by the Americans, Cornwallis had little choice but to give up. "We at that time could not fire a single gun," he would later write.

It is said that the British played the tune "The World Turned Upside Down" when they marched to lay down their arms.

Whether or not that's true, it makes for a good story and certainly mirrored their despair.

The Yorktown battleground today is part of the Colonial National Historical Park, which includes a grand Georgian mansion called the Nelson House (built in 1730), where Cornwallis lived with his officers. Nearby is the Moore House, where surrender negotiations took place. Cornwallis refused to relinquish his sword to Washington and instead sent Brigadier General Charles O'Hara. The Yorktown grounds also contain a museum (in a somewhat undistinguished brick building), and the house where Washington had his headquarters. A row of cannons is on display outdoors, some of which were ten-pounders.

"Such a scene of sorrow and weeping I had never before witnessed."

Washington's Adieu

FRAUNCES TAVERN · New York City

ID George Washington ever crack a bad joke? Roll his eyes? Whisper sweet nothings? Of course he did. But it's difficult to imagine. I've read many biographies of Washington, but I rarely find the man inside the general or the president. The other Founding Fathers are different. John Adams seems less mysterious. His letters to Abigail are full of feeling. Jefferson, despite his imposing intellect, strikes me as down-to-earth. And as for other former presidents, I could envision Lincoln slapping his knee, playing a prank, or tripping over his own feet.

Washington is an enigma. It may be that, like many Americans, I have trouble seeing anything beyond the unflinching stoicism portrayed by movie stars from Gary Cooper to Daniel Craig. It's possible that we'd know more about Washington's inner life if we had more of his letters. But Martha burned them, with the exception of two, after he died, to keep their relationship private, as was the custom of the time.

What we do have, however, is Fraunces Tavern, and that's where we know Washington showed genuine emotion. During his final meeting with his officers, witnesses saw a side of the commander in chief that was rarely visible. The date was December 4, 1783, at the end of the Revolution, and a large room at the tavern had been chosen for a celebration. After dinner,

Washington raised his glass and gave a toast: "With a heart full of love and gratitude, I now take leave of you. I most devoutly wish that your later days may be as prosperous and happy as your former ones have been glorious and honorable. I cannot … I cannot come to each of you but shall feel obliged if each of you will come and take me by the hand."

Major Benjamin Tallmadge, who was an intelligence officer, recorded in his diary how the officers came forth one by one: "General Knox being nearest to him [Washington] turned to the Commander-in-chief who, suffused in tears, was incapable of utterance but grasped his hand when they embraced each other in silence. In the same affectionate manner every officer in the room marched up and parted with his general in chief. Such a scene of sorrow and weeping I had never before witnessed and fondly hope I may never be called to witness again."

There was little that Knox, in particular, had not done for his superior. He directed rebel artillery fire at the Battle of Bunker Hill; he led the transport of heavy cannons three hundred miles from Fort Ticonderoga; and he was in charge of logistics for crossing the Delaware before the Battle of Trenton. For his dedicated service, when Washington became president, he would make Knox his secretary of war.

It is possible today to visit the New York site—if not the original structure—where this farewell dinner took place. Fraunces Tavern is in the Financial District, about twenty blocks in either direction from Freedom Tower and the Brooklyn Bridge. It's a Colonial, redbrick building, and though a replica of the original, it's a convincing one. Washington would be hard-pressed to tell the difference. Built in 1904, seventy years after the original was burned, the tavern stands at the corner of Pearl and Broad Streets. It looks tiny now compared to the megatowers nearby, but it was once the tallest building on the block. During the early years of America's emerging republic, the tavern was used as the Department of Foreign Affairs and the Department of the Treasury. And in 1804 the Society of Cincinnati hosted a dinner honoring veteran officers that was attended by both Alexander Hamilton and Aaron Burr, only weeks before their duel.

My first visit to Fraunces Tavern was once again with Fred Cookinham, the professional tour guide who also led me through the Morris-Jumel Mansion and Hamilton Grange. Fred met me outside the building one afternoon in July 2018. He was standing in front of a bronze plaque that identified the building as a National Landmark. Fred started to tell me about the history of the surrounding area as it was during Washington's time but the clamor of honking traffic made it tough to hear him.

"The tavern was started in 1762 by a man named Samuel Fraunces," he said, raising his voice. "He called it the Queen's Head Tavern, named for England's queen Charlotte. It was later changed to Fraunces. The streets here were quite different then. A canal existed just in front of the tavern, and you can still see a dip in the topography where the water ran. Look over there. See the little dell where Pearl Street runs?"

I squinted and tried to envision the streetscape without neon signs and walls of glass.

"This area downtown, near where the Twin Towers fell," continued Fred, "was what was then New York City. Buildings were cheek by jowl, no more than a few stories high, many of them hugging the shoreline of the two flanking bodies of water, the Hudson and the East River. The structures were built along the natural contours of the landscape rather than imposed on an artificial grid. Most of the remaining sections of the island, north of here, was farmland. In some cases, there were large estates in what is now Central Park and Upper Manhattan. Because the main part of the city was built around the port, you could look out from the tavern's windows and see a forest of masts and sails."

I asked Fred what he knew of the tavern's reconstruction.

"The Sons of the Revolution bought the lot in 1883 and rebuilt the tavern, based on plans and etchings from the time. You can see the reconstructed Flemish bond brickwork that was common in the 1700s."

I stepped forward and touched the masonry. It may have not been original, but it felt old and crusty. Flakes of brick dust came off on my hands. Stepping back from the curb, I noticed the rows of twelve-by-twelve windows and the hipped roof crowned by a wooden balustrade. Two dormers were visible, anchored by a tall chimney. We passed through the front door, up a few stone steps, and crossed the threshold into the restaurant. There were chipped paint and smudges on the walls and moldings. I wondered if they were left that way intentionally. By the bar were high wooden stools. Trestle tables filled the rest of the room.

I took a moment to peruse the menu. It listed several colonial-era dishes: raw oysters, fish-and-chips, liver pâté, lamb stew, chicken potpie. Some other selections were "Jefferson's Cobb Salad," "George Washington Horseback" (an appetizer of bacon, dates, and almonds), and "Scotch Egg" (a sausage blend of porter, cheddar, and local honey). Older menus on the wall, among them one from 1907, listed English mutton chop, "Consommé Martha," roast stuffed duckling, pickled walnuts, minced chicken, calf's head, and buttered beets and onions.

Resisting the temptation to sit down and eat, Fred and I headed up to the second floor. There Fred showed me the Long Room, which was furnished to resemble the one Washington used for his farewell to his officers. A large rectilinear wooden table, with Windsor chairs, was set neatly with pewter utensils and plates. Fred said that each December a reenactment takes place with an actor portraying Washington.

Recently that actor has been Ian Kahn, who played Washington in the 2017 AMC series *Turn: Washington's Spies*. Kahn, who is six feet tall, is quoted on the tavern's website as saying that he added an extra inch to the bottom of his heels to match Washington's height.

"This reenactment is very popular," said Fred. "It costs one dollar to reserve a ticket and includes a selfie with the actor."

Fred and I went on to see the other rooms in the tavern, one of which housed a small but informative museum display. There was a letter from the Patriot spy Nathan Hale; a portrait of DeWitt Clinton; a painting of Mary Ludwig Hays, who helped rebel soldiers load cannons during the Battle of Monmouth; and a collection of Dutch smoking pipes from the days of New Amsterdam, in the 1600s.

Back out on Pearl Street, Fred and I parted ways. I took another look at the sea of taxis, overflowing garbage cans, and towering skyscrapers and imagined what Washington might have thought. Maybe he'd have said, somewhat horrified, "What have they done to my country?" He was human, after all.

At the same time, though, he might have felt nostalgic for that moment when he was remembered so affectionately by his soldiers in arms, a moment that brought him to tears.

Franklin never lost his love for ink and fonts.

A Man for All Seasons

FRANKLIN COURT PRINTING OFFICE
Philadelphia, Pennsylvania

MY GREAT-UNCLE Carl Van Doren was a noted historian. He wrote many books about American history, including *The Secret History of the American Revolution* (1941), *Mutiny in January* (1943), and *The Great Rehearsal* (1948), but it was his biography of Benjamin Franklin that made his name. It was a best seller and won the Pulitzer Prize in 1939. Over the next decade, Carl would continue writing about Franklin. In 1950 he even published a biography of Franklin's sister, Jane Mecom. "We used to joke as a family," Carl's daughter Barbara once told me, "that Dad was so into Franklin that he was beginning to look like him!"

But is it a wonder that Carl was fascinated by Franklin? The Sage of Philadelphia, as he is sometimes known, was a homegrown Leonardo: an inventor, statesman, author, scientist, printer, publisher. He invented the Franklin stove, bifocals, the glass harmonica, the lightning rod; he created the first public library and the first fire company. He was, as Carl wrote, "a harmonious, human multitude."

Franklin was also one of our best-known and most eminent Founding Fathers. He was a signer of both the Declaration of Independence and the Constitution (one of only six to do so). He helped draft early grievances against Parliament and brought them to a wider audience in the *Pennsylvania Gazette* (which he founded). It was Franklin who championed Thomas Paine and encouraged him to come to America and it was Franklin, as ambassador to France, who, among others, persuaded the French to become an ally.

But for all Franklin's accomplishments, there are few historic sites that bring him to life. There is no Mount Vernon, no Monticello, no Peacefield. His house in Philadelphia was demolished long ago; in its place is a modern, steel-frame reconstruction that outlines its original silhouette. This "sculpture" was designed in 1976 by the architect Robert Venturi and is admirable as a concept, but it doesn't reveal much about who Franklin was.

Was there another site that could shed more light? In fall 2019, I went looking. My quest led me to Yale University's Sterling Library, in New Haven. There I discovered on an upper floor a little-known library-within-a-library called the Franklin Papers. Entering Room 230, I found a large space filled with hundreds of rare books carefully arranged on wooden shelves. The room was seemingly empty of humans. I took a moment to walk around and inspect the worn, fragile-looking volumes, many with chipped bindings and flaking pages. On a center table I saw a bust of Franklin, a copy of Houdon's famous sculpture done from life. More images of Franklin in paintings and etchings were hung high on the walls. What a treasure this collection was! I wondered where to start my research.

As I was perusing the card catalog—a rare commodity in the digital age—I heard a woman's voice behind me: "May I help you?"

I turned around: "Oh, yes," I said, feeling sheepish for snooping. "I'm looking for information about historic sites associated with Franklin."

"Well, you've come to the right place," she said. "Please, come sit down. I'm Ellen Cohn, the editor of the collection." I pulled up a chair beside her, and she asked if I was related to Carl Van Doren. "Of all the bios on Franklin, his is still the standard," she said, which pleased me no end.

"This space was designed originally to be the Classics Library," Ellen said, "but when Yale received this collection as a gift, it changed its plans. Yale alum William Smith Mason spent forty years assembling these materials and gave them to Yale in the 1930s." Franklin's connection to Yale, I learned, dates back to 1753, when the university conferred on him an honorary master's degree.

Ellen had been working at the Collection for forty-one years. "I began as a researcher, and I guess I never left," she said. Ellen studied at Wesleyan University in the 1970s, where she wrote her thesis on the history of the sea shanties that sailors sang during the heyday of New England whaling.

"What a great place to work!" I said, looking at her desk and stained-glass windows behind her. They were decorated with images from Greek and Roman mythology and Aesop's Fables. One was of "The Proud Frog"; another, "The Argonaut."

"The collection," she continued, "has more than fifteen thousand volumes. His papers are a real door into the eighteenth century. Currently I'm working on a set of documents about Franklin's time in Paris. He spent all the years of the Revolution there. He went with John Adams for a while, but the two didn't get along. I'm sure Adams wasn't happy that the French were more enamored with Franklin than with him. Franklin was a hero to Parisians, especially for his electrical discoveries like the lightning rod. He had been elected to the French Academy of Science, which was quite an accomplishment for an American."

Ellen adjusted some books on her desk, which was piled high with papers. "The Continental Congress," she said, "following the Battles of Lexington and Concord in 1775, agreed to send Franklin to France to muster support for the war. They signed a Treaty of Alliance in 1778. From 1778 through 1782, France continued to provide the Continental Army with troops, ammunition, warships, and uniforms."

She shifted gears for a moment and concentrated on the reason for my visit. She seemed deep in thought. "Hm," she said. "As to sites you can explore, associated with Franklin, I think the best choice would be his old print shop in Philadelphia. It's in the original building. Franklin thought of himself as a printer first and foremost. He set up the shop so that his grandson Benjamin Franklin Bache could learn the trade."

She continued: "Franklin came back from Paris after the Revolution in 1785 and planned to take it easy, but it didn't happen. He was always brimming with ideas. He decided to buy the two buildings near him that bordered Market Street in Philadelphia and set up the print shop. He also designed an archway, which leads you toward what was then his house. It's now called Franklin Court."

If you visit the print shop today, a Park Ranger will show you how the instruments of printing were used in Franklin's day. Sometimes interesting documents are printed there, as was the case when I visited. It was a facsimile of the last letter Washington wrote to Franklin, on September 23, 1789. It reads: "If to be venerated for benevolence, if to be admired for talents, if to be esteemed for patriotism . . . can gratify the human mind, you must have the pleasing consolation to know that you did not live in vain . . . so long as I retain my memory, you will be recollected with respect, veneration, and affection, by your sincere friend, George Washington."

Franklin's role as a printer was crucial to uniting the colonies. Even years before the Revolution—during the French and Indian War—he printed a cartoon in the *Pennsylvania Gazette* (the colonies' most influential paper) of a snake cut into thirteen pieces, symbolizing the thirteen colonies. It was captioned "Join or Die," and was meant to warn of French intruders who were infiltrating the Ohio River Valley. The cartoon "went viral," and was revived during the Revolution to drum up support for a united front against British rule.

Ellen Cohn is an expert on Franklin as a printer. "I belong to the Society of Printers, which meets once a year in Boston," she said. "I've given a few talks there and will give one next year on Franklin's knowledge of printing money." She then started rummaging through her desk to find a sample font from her letterpress printing collection that would have been used by Franklin. She found fonts designed by both Caslon and Baskerville.

Just before I left, Ellen mentioned additional Franklin sites worth visiting—the Franklin Museum in Philadelphia ("a bit lightweight, however, for the more serious historian") and the Franklin Institute in Philadelphia ("which has a large statue of Franklin sculpted by James Earle Fraser").

"There's Franklin's grave, too," she said, "which is not far from Independence Hall. If you visit it, note the epitaph, which he composed himself. It says simply: Franklin, Printer."

This august edifice is where Washington left his mark on a fledgling nation.

A Noble Gesture

MARYLAND STATE HOUSE · *Annapolis, Maryland*
CAPITOL ROTUNDA · *Washington, D.C.*

A REMARKABLE THING happened on December 23, 1783, in Annapolis, Maryland. It may not rival Bunker Hill or Yorktown, but it was a touchstone for American democracy. There were no musket balls, bayonet attacks, or cavalry charges. By comparison, it was a subdued affair: Here, on that date, George Washington resigned his military commission.

If you're wondering why this was remarkable, it's understandable. It sounds about as interesting as renewing your driver's license. And, yes, it was essentially a piece of paperwork. But, in the end, it was the principle, not the action, that was historic. To establish the context: The Revolution had just ended, and Washington had emerged a national hero. Congress had already made plans to honor him with commissioned sculptures. There was even talk of making him a king, as ironic as that seems for a new republic.

But Washington would have none of it. He was content that he had fulfilled his duty as a general. The historian Thomas Fleming noted in his book *First in Their Hearts: The Life of George Washington* (1991): "The man who could have dispersed a feckless Congress and obtained for himself and his officers riches worthy of their courage was renouncing absolute power to become a private citizen."

Like Cincinnatus, the hero who wanted to return to his farm after fighting for Rome, Washington wanted to retire to his plantation at Mount Vernon. For his humility, Washington would receive praise from none other than King George III, who reportedly told the American-born artist Benjamin West: "If Washington does that [resigns his commission], he will be the greatest man in the world."

Washington's actual resignation was a formal ceremony at the State House. It followed carefully prescribed protocol but was not without celebration. There were dinners, speeches, and dancing—at which Washington excelled. According to the Delaware delegate James Tilton, "The General danced every set, that all the ladies might have the pleasure of dancing with him, or as it has since been handsomely expressed, *get a touch of him.*"

The following morning, a more somber gathering took place, arranged by a committee comprising Thomas Jefferson, James McHenry (a Maryland statesman), and Elbridge Gerry (a former member of the Continental Congress). As Tilton described it: "At twelve o'clock the General was introduced by the Secretary, and seated opposite to the president . . . The ladies occupied the gallery as full as it would hold. Silence ordered, by the Secretary, the Genl. rose and bowed to congress, who uncovered, but did not bow. He then delivered his speech, and at the close of it drew his commission from his bosom and handed it to the president."

Molly Ridout, one of the women in the gallery, wrote in a letter to her mother a few years later that "the General seemed so much affected himself that everybody felt for him. He addressed Congress in a short Speech but very affecting. Many tears were shed . . . I think the World never produced a greater man & very few so good."

Ridout's and Tilson's recollections are vivid, but ironically it was someone who was not present—and more than three thousand miles away—who would leave the most impressive record. John Trumbull, an artist who had fought in the Revolution, was in London when Washington resigned as commander in chief. He considered the moment to be "one of the highest moral lessons ever given to the world." Thirty-seven years after the event, he was commissioned by Congress to a paint scene of it, as imagined from existing accounts. In the painting *General George Washington Resigning His Commission* (1824), Trumbull depicts Washington in full military uniform as he addresses the Continental Congress. Among the figures in the picture are Colonel Benjamin Walker, a captain and member of Washington's staff; Thomas Mifflin, president of the Continental Congress; Charles Thomson, secretary of the Continental Congress; Martha Washington; and future presidents Thomas Jefferson, James Monroe, and James Madison, who were then delegates.

Today, Trumbull's work hangs in the rotunda of the United States Capitol. The canvas is almost eighteen feet long; a smaller version hangs in the Yale University Art Gallery. For those who prefer sculpture, there's a bronze of Washington at full scale in the State House's Old Senate Chamber, which has been restored to its original appearance when Congress met there in 1783.

In another room of the State House, Washington's handwritten speech is on exhibit in a state-of-the-art display case that preserves the 237-year-old address, now considered to be one of the most important documents in American history. "Having now finished the work assigned to me," he wrote in one passage, "I retire from the great theatre of Action."

Poignant words that remind us of the significance—and fragility—of one of America's most important symbols of democracy: the peaceful transfer of power.

Paine ponders the nearby grounds of his former New York estate.

Voice of the People

THOMAS PAINE PLAQUE · *New York City*
THOMAS PAINE MONUMENT
New Rochelle, New York

I N THE heart of New York's Greenwich Village, off Sheridan Square, is a bar called Marie's Crisis Café. It was founded in the 1850s and was once a house of ill repute. More important to us, though, it was the roominghouse in which Thomas Paine, the author of *Common Sense*, died, in 1809. (An earlier pamphlet was titled *The American Crisis*; hence, the name of the bar.) On the outside wall there's a bronze plaque commemorating Paine. It's easy to miss—I'd passed it many times before noticing it one night while visiting the jazz club Arthur's Tavern, next door.

On the plaque is a portrait of Paine in bas-relief with a border carved with quotes from his essays:

I BELIEVE IN ONE GOD AND NO MORE;

THE WORLD IS MY COUNTRY;

ALL MANKIND ARE MY BRETHREN;

TO DO GOOD IS MY RELIGION

At the bottom the marker reads: THIS TABLET WAS PLACED ON JUNE 9, 1923, BY THE GREENWICH VILLAGE HISTORICAL SOCIETY.

What the plaque doesn't tell us is that Paine died penniless and forgotten. How he ended up that way speaks to a tempestuous life. At his height, Paine was one of the most successful authors in American history. *Common Sense*, which vehemently argued for independence, sold 350,000 copies. Given the population of the colonies at that time—about 2.5 million—that number is extraordinary.

But in hindsight the question arises: "What was new in this small volume that sparked such interest?" After all, Paine's ideas weren't original. What *was* original, however, was how he expressed them. Unlike much writing of the time, Paine's prose was accessible—it didn't contain references to the Greek philosophers whom Adams and Jefferson so often cited. It contained lively similes and metaphors: "Government, like dress, is the badge of lost innocence; the palaces of kings are built on the ruins of the bowers of paradise."

And stirring passages: "Small islands, not capable of protecting themselves, are the proper objects for kingdoms to take under their care; but there is something absurd, in supposing a continent to be perpetually governed by an island."

The way he expressed his moral and political arguments for America's freedom resonated with colonists. John Adams was so taken with *Common Sense* that he wrote to his wife, "I could not have written any Thing in so manly and striking a style." George Washington, too, admired Paine's work and read it to his troops before the crossing of the Delaware. And Benjamin Franklin, who met Paine in September 1774 in London, where Paine was advocating for social causes, was one of the first to suggest he come to America. Shortly thereafter, Paine was sailing for the colonies. His first stop would be Philadelphia, where he began his crusade for independence.

But for all Paine's influence, he was a difficult man to like. He made enemies easily, even eventually turning against Washington and calling him elitist and incompetent. His provocative *Age of Reason* (1794), which was considered blasphemous because it attacked organized religion, also alienated him from the general public.

Paine did not have an easy childhood. He was born in 1737 in Thetford, England, to a poor family. His father, Joseph, was a tenant farmer and stay-maker with few prospects. Thomas worked brief stints as a sailor, a tax official, and a teacher, and failed at all of them. Dispirited, he found in America a place where he could channel his frustrations about social change into his writings. He proclaimed that the British system—based on a monarchy and tyrannical aristocracy—was fundamentally flawed.

Paine argued that the colonies should abandon England once and for all, create a democratic government with a written constitution, and reap the advantages of free trade. Americans were persuaded.

After the Revolution, Paine returned to England and in 1791 published the *Rights of Man*, which advocated, among other ideas, that a nation should replace its government if it failed to serve the people. Written in part as a critical response to Edmund Burke's condemnation of the French Revolution, it sold more than a million copies. Soon, though, Paine was charged with seditious libel because the government of Prime Minister William Pitt was fearful that this book would incite a revolution in Britain. Paine escaped to France in 1793 before he could be tried. There he also caused controversy. His opposition to the beheading of Louis XVI and his insistence on France adopting a constitution landed him in jail. It took America's ambassador to France, James Monroe, eleven months to negotiate his release so he could return to the United States. In the ensuing years, Paine would focus his efforts and money on pursuing ill-fated inventions, including a smokeless candle and a design for an iron bridge.

There is a more substantial memorial to Paine in New Rochelle, New York, a suburb of eighty thousand. During Paine's time, this area of Westchester County had only seven hundred residents and was mostly farmland. In 1802, Paine lived there on a 277-acre estate that was awarded to him by the New York State legislature for his services to the American cause.

The monument was the idea of a New York publisher, Gilbert Vale, in 1905, and was funded through public subscription. The modest-size bust, created by the artist James Wilson MacDonald, sits on a tall stone plinth surrounded by an iron gate.

Paine died a bitter man, feeling misunderstood and underappreciated. The world had become too much for him. Jill Lepore in an article in *The New Yorker* in 2019, writes: "A neighbor of Paine's came across the old man in a tavern in New Rochelle, so drunk and disoriented and unkempt that his toenails had grown over his toes, like bird's claws . . . Paine hobbled to the polls in New Rochelle to cast his vote in a local election. He was told that he was not an American citizen and was turned away. So much for the rights of man."

Even a street name honoring him in New York City was changed. A plaque on Barrow Street, not far from where he died, notes that "Barrow" was originally called "Reason Street," after Paine's *Age of Reason*, but as Paine faded from memory, common usage corrupted "Reason Street" to "Raisin Street." In 1828 the street was renamed in honor of the artist Thomas Barrow (1770–1825).

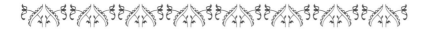

Hero of the Sea

CRYPT OF JOHN PAUL JONES,
UNITED STATES NAVAL ACADEMY
Annapolis, Maryland
JOHN PAUL JONES HISTORIC HOUSE MUSEUM
Portsmouth, New Hampshire

JOHN PAUL Jones is straight out of a Walter Mitty fantasy. His daring exploits, like those in James Thurber's imaginings, are larger than life. They're the kind that keep schoolboys up at night, imagining raids, narrow escapes, pirates, mutinies. "I have not yet begun to fight!" was Jones's immortal cry. Over the years his legend has grown, and though some of his feats have been exaggerated, he remains an important figure from the Revolution.

Jones had a brash temperament, no doubt stemming from a rugged childhood in rural Scotland. In 1760, at the age of twelve, he set out as a sailor on the high seas. He would soon advance from cabin boy on a merchant vessel, to chief mate on a slaver brigantine, to master on a Scottish clipper ship. By 1774, he had found his way to Philadelphia to volunteer his services to the Revolutionary cause. As a senior lieutenant in the new Continental Navy, he made a name for himself in battles against British frigates in the Atlantic from Bermuda to Nova Scotia.

The artist N. C. Wyeth captured this heroic figure in his 1938 painting *Captain John Paul Jones.* Jones is shown on deck, saber in hand, while smoke billows from his ship and torn sails flap in the wind. A young sailor is at his feet, ready to fire a cannon. The true-life Jones was just as dashing. His triumph over the British man-of-war the *Serapis* was a David-and-Goliath story: Even as his smaller frigate was sinking, he managed to jump aboard the enemy vessel and win the day. His ship, the *Bonhomme Richard*, had been crippled by several broadsides from the *Serapis*, and within an hour it had sunk to the bottom of the sea.

But if Jones's escapades were so triumphant, why did he die a forgotten man? I wanted to learn more. I made a trip to the United States Naval Academy, in Annapolis, Maryland, where Jones is entombed (he had originally been buried in a pauper's grave in Paris). Set on the Chesapeake Bay, Annapolis is known for its colonial architecture, such as the James Brice House and the Upton Scott House. The Naval Academy, perhaps the city's most famous institution, is situated on the port. Its impressive campus boasts a domed chapel that was built in 1912 by Ernest Flagg. Beneath the chapel, in the crypt, is where Jones lies.

Four stone columns guard a sarcophagus carved in veined black-and-white marble. Elaborately sculpted dolphins surround the base. The overall design was created by Whitney Warren, a Beaux-Arts architect who also designed New York City's Grand Central Station. The tomb is an exercise in gaudy excess, but Jones would likely have approved. He thought well of himself.

But questions about Jones still remained for me. I did some research and contacted the journalist and historian Evan Thomas, whose book *John Paul Jones* was published in 2003. Thomas, based in Washington, D.C., is a former editor of *Newsweek* (1985–99) and the author of a best-selling book on Richard Nixon. He agreed to meet with me in New York City, and we set a date in December 2019 to get together for coffee at EJ's

Luncheonette, on the Upper East Side. Thomas was in town to moderate a discussion at the Council on Foreign Relations with Tom Brokaw and Henry Kissinger, but he made time to squeeze me in.

"How did you land on Jones as a subject?"

"Well, for one thing, I'm an avid sailor, so Jones's life at sea was compelling to me. Also, Jones was an enigma and full of contradictions. He was a hero but a complex one."

Evan explained that although Jones won the early support of people like Washington and Benjamin Franklin, he could be belligerent and rebellious. I thought of another hardheaded patriot, Thomas Paine.

"Jones was ambitious and wanted the status of a gentleman officer," Thomas said. "He came from a humble background and becoming a naval officer was a way to rise up."

Evan visited Jones's boyhood home in Scotland while re- searching his book and was intrigued by what he discovered. "His father, Blake Paul, was a gardener for the Arbigland estate," he told me, "but he was more like a landscape designer." Some of his garden plans, Evan suggested, might have impressed Ca- pability Brown, the designer of such estates as Blenheim Palace, one of England's grandest houses from the eighteenth century.

"And by the way, John Paul Jones was not his real name. It was just 'John Paul,'" the author said. "He added 'Jones' to mask his identity; he was on the run after killing a man who had tried to lead a mutiny on his ship. In the end, Jones got off on self-defense."

"What was his greatest legacy?" I asked.

"Well, for one, he was fearless," Evan answered. "And he gave the Americans some semblance of a navy when it had none. Jones's small fleet was no match for the British armada, but he could give them trouble by randomly attacking them in their waters. He was kind of a modern-day terrorist."

Evan Thomas, a tall, thin man with short straight hair and glasses, was in his sixties and very fit. He looked as if he could sail a schooner with the next favorable wind. I asked him what battle Jones is best known for.

He answered quickly: "The defeat of the *Serapis*, definitely. Jones had been pestering the French—then an American ally—to give him a large vessel. And he got one. But it was a worn-out frigate that was barely seaworthy. Jones gave it a new name: the *Bonhomme Richard*, after Ben Franklin's *Poor Richard's Almanac*. It was a tribute to his friend and champion."

Evan expounded on the battle with the *Serapis*. "Jones won by launching a torch that set fire to the ship. The triumph won him instant fame. He became a celebrity in France."

"Where did he live in America?"

"In Portsmouth, New Hampshire. But he didn't stay there long. He was there for only a couple of years while overseeing the construction of the *America*, the first ship-of-the-line built for the Continental Army. The house is a museum now. Nearby there's a replica of one of the ships Jones sailed on. I took an excursion on it, but I was disappointed by how slow it was, only a few knots."

After the Revolutionary War, Jones's contentious nature caught up with him. He felt underappreciated by the powers that be, who failed to promote him sufficiently (as he perceived it), and he sought employment elsewhere. He became a mercenary for Catherine the Great of Russia. His service was short-lived, though, because he was accused of raping a ten-year-old girl. The accusation was not proved (according to Russian law he would have been beheaded), but the damage to his reputation was done and Jones would die an outcast.

"Teddy Roosevelt was the one who really helped elevate

The Bonhomme Richard *rides the waves toward her finest hour.*

Jones's reputation," Evan Thomas said. "Roosevelt wanted to draw attention to the navy, which he hoped to raise funds for, and he fought for a monument to Jones that might spark interest with Congress. The sculpture was over the top, but it worked."

I pulled out a copy of Evans's book on Jones and asked him to sign it. We left the restaurant together and I accompanied him till we got to East Sixty-eighth Street, home of the Council on Foreign Relations. A crowd was already gathering, but I had no interest in hanging around for a glimpse of celebrities. Evan and I said goodbye.

As I walked back up toward Park Avenue, I opened up the Thomas book to read his inscription. The din of blaring horns in Manhattan was in the background as I read the words: "To Adam, a fellow traveler—walk the battlefield!"

Appendices

Paul Revere rides his mare Brown Beauty.

Additional Landmarks Noted in Brief

✣

THE MONTGOMERY MONUMENT · *St. Paul's Chapel, New York City*

In Lower Manhattan, just a few blocks from the Freedom Tower, stands St. Paul's Chapel, where Washington worshipped when he lived in New York. Above its east window is a memorial to Richard Montgomery, the first general officer killed in the Revolution (at Quebec). The monument was commissioned by the Continental Congress in 1776 and was sculpted in France by Jean-Jacques Caffieri, under the direction of Benjamin Franklin. Montgomery fought for the British army during the French and Indian War, but when the Revolution broke out, he joined the Patriot cause.

PAUL REVERE STATUE · *Boston, Massachusetts*

Paul Revere was largely forgotten after his death, in 1818. It would take an 1861 poem by Longfellow to revive his name: "Listen, my children, and you shall hear / Of the midnight ride of Paul Revere." It took take another eighty-one years for Revere to get a real biography. Esther Forbes's 1941 book was a best-seller and Revere was news again. The frontispiece featured Copley's painting of Revere holding a silver bowl. Indeed, he was a noted silversmith, but he was also a printer, officer, leader of a spy ring, amateur dentist, and a maker of bells, producing some nine hundred of them. One still rings in King's Chapel, in Boston, not far from the Old North Church, where a statue of Revere by Cyrus Edwin Dallin stands in the square.

MINUTE MAN NATIONAL PARK · *Lexington, Massachusetts*

In the early hours of April 19, 1775, in Lexington, Massachusetts, Jonas Parker, a Minute Man (the "first responder" of the day), was among seventy men who assembled on the town green. The British were marching seven hundred regulars to neighboring Concord to raid munition stores. The rebels were allegedly given an order by Colonel William Prescott: "Don't fire until you the see the whites of their eyes!" A shot was fired (whose, we will never know) and then another. Parker was the first to fall. He and his fellow Patriots are remembered at Minute Man Historical Park, with a commemorative statue sculpted in 1900 by Henry Kitson. Another statue, at Concord (by Daniel Chester French), recalls lines from an Emerson poem: "Here once the embattled farmers stood / And fired the shot heard round the world."

CARPENTERS' HALL · *Philadelphia, Pennsylvania*
When most of us think of undercover agents and covert operations, we think of the CIA or the KGB. But organized "intelligence-gathering" also existed during the American Revolution. In 1775 the Second Continental Congress created a Committee of Secret Correspondence, comprising Benjamin Franklin, Benjamin Harrison, Thomas Johnson, and James Lovell, who was an expert on codes and ciphers. One of their historic meetings took place at Carpenters' Hall in 1777, when a French spy named Bonvouloir joined them and provided critical information to aid the Americans against Britain. Today, you can visit the building, a beautifully proportioned brick edifice, which is also where a seven-week session of the First Continental Congress met in 1774.

CITY OF SAVANNAH · *Georgia*
The oldest city in Georgia was the site of a major Revolutionary War conflict. During the Siege of Boston, in 1775, the British were short of provisions, so they sent a fleet to Savannah to secure them (particularly rice). The colonial Georgia Council of Safety assumed the city was under attack and arrested British Royal Governor James Wright. The Battle of the Rice Boats

took place on March 2–3, 1776, and the British were forced out. They would regain the city, however, in 1778, and control it for most of the rest of the war.

PRISON SHIP MARTYRS' MONUMENT · *Fort Greene, New York*
One of the darkest chapters of the Revolution concerned the horrific treatment of American prisoners by the British. Thousands of captives were held on decommissioned ships anchored in Wallabout Bay, near New York City. Many were soldiers but others had been apprehended simply because they refused to swear allegiance to the Crown. More than eleven thousand five hundred died of overcrowding, contaminated water, starvation, and disease. In 1908 a monument to these martyrs, designed by Stanford White, was dedicated by President Taft.

BRANDYWINE BATTLEFIELD · *Chadds Ford, Pennsylvania*
Growing up, one of my favorite books was a volume of Andrew Wyeth's paintings, *Wyeth at Kuerners*, published in 1972, which contains his landscapes of Chadds Ford. For many years, I associated this region only with Wyeth. Recently, I discovered that it was also the site of the Battle of Brandywine (1777). In 2019 I took a tour of the site with guide Andrew Outten. We met in a house Washington used as headquarters. Outten explained that Washington lost because he was outwitted by Cornwallis, who surprised the rebels' rear flank by crossing an unguarded ford. As I left the house, I noticed a large sycamore in the front. It was same one I'd first seen so many years ago in Wyeth's tempera painting *Pennsylvania Landscape* (1942).

THE HALES-BYRNES HOUSE · *Newark, Delaware*
In 1777 Washington stayed at this residence, which is now on the Washington-Rochambeau National Historic Trail, but not merely for tea and lodgings. On September 6 the general and

his high command—Nathaniel Greene, Henry Knox, John Sullivan, William Maxwell, Anthony Wayne, and the Marquis de Lafayette—met here to plan a counteroffensive against the British, who were gunning for Philadelphia. The ensuing battle, at Brandywine, was a Cornwallis victory, and the British would occupy the city for much of the war.

VAN CORTLANDT HOUSE MUSEUM · *Bronx, New York*
Off the Hudson River Parkway, just beyond Manhattan, is the oldest-surviving house in the Bronx. It originally belonged to Frederick Van Cortlandt (1699–1749), and was twice a temporary home for Washington, in 1776 and 1783. It was also used by the Comte de Rochambeau and the Marquis de Lafayette. Designed in the Georgian style, the house was built by Africans enslaved by Van Cortlandt. In summer 2019 I took a tour with "historical interpreter" Michael Grillo, who sometimes plays the role of Washington in local reenactments.

SARATOGA BATTLEFIELD · *Saratoga, New York*
In a cloister at Westminster Abbey in London, there's a stone tablet set in the masonry floor. It bears the inscription JOHN BURGOYNE 1722–1792, nothing more. For 150 years his grave lay unmarked; it wasn't until 1963 that the name was finally chiseled into place. "Gentleman Johnny" Burgoyne, as he was known, had once been a celebrated general in the British army, but his crushing defeat at Saratoga, at the hands of Benedict Arnold, ruined his name. I spoke on the phone with Colonel Sean Scully, a history professor at West Point, in 2020: "Every year I take my students to Saratoga to see the monument to Arnold," he told me. "There's no name on it, given that he was a traitor; there's only a bas-relief of a boot because he was wounded in the foot."

GILBERT STUART HOMESTEAD · *Saunders, Rhode Island*

Gilbert Stuart was not a Founding Father, but he painted portraits of many of them. His long list of subjects include John and Abigail Adams, John Jay, Thomas Jefferson, James Madison, James Monroe, Martha Washington, and George Washington, whom he painted more than a hundred times. During one sitting, when the artist offered to talk with the taciturn general about horses and farming, Washington lit up. "Soon Stuart's brush," wrote the historian Thomas Flexner, "flew merrily in rhythm with his tongue." The result is what now appears on the dollar bill. Stuart's birthplace, which was once a working snuff mill, is now a house museum.

NATHANAEL GREENE HOUSE · *Warwick, Rhode Island*

I think it's safe to say that if Washington had been asked to name his most trusted general, he'd immediately have replied: "Nathanael Greene." Greene played key roles in the Battles of Germantown and Brandywine and the Siege of Boston. But perhaps his greatest contribution was in the southern campaign, when he managed, against great odds, to keep Cornwallis at bay and finally cornered him at Yorktown. You may not know Greene's name, but I recommend a visit to this historic site. The restored antique house sits on some five acres, and in the front yard, now fully grown, there's a tree that had been planted in memory of George Washington. But it's not a cherry tree.

LAFAYETTE STATUE · *Lafayette Park, Washington, D.C.*

Parades, front-page news, souvenir books, commemorative plates—no, this wasn't the arrival of the Beatles. It was 1824, and the Marquis de Lafayette had returned to America. It was an unprecedented celebration of a conquering hero, a revered general and friend of George Washington's, on the fiftieth anniversary of America's independence. The marquis had been a commander at Yorktown and Brandywine and was a passionate champion of democracy. A statue of him, designed by Alexander Falguière and Antonin Mercié, was erected in 1891.

PORTRAIT OF BENJAMIN RUSH · *National Portrait Gallery, Washington, D.C.*
Benjamin Rush was in his time one of the most famous Founding Fathers, although perhaps few of us ever heard of him. In addition to being a noted physician and the "Father of Psychiatry," he was a signer of the Declaration of Independence, founder of Dickinson College, a professor of chemistry, and an organizer of an antislavery society. He was equally at home on the battlefield (as a surgeon) as he was in the halls of Congress. Sadly, the house in Philadelphia where he was born was demolished. At the National Portrait Gallery, however, there's a handsome portrait (1812) of Rush by Thomas Sully. The distinguished doctor is shown with a pensive gaze, wondering perhaps why he's not better known.

LINDLEY'S MILL · *Orange County, North Carolina*
Many years ago, I restored a nineteenth century grist mill on my family's property in Connecticut. Fast forward thirty years to 2018, and I was talking with my friend Lindley Young. She told me of a little known skirmish during the Revolution called the Battle of Lindley's Mill. Naturally, I was interested. "It's in North Carolina, where I was born," she said. "It still exists, and I am a direct relation to the original mill owners." She told me the battle was fought between patriots and loyalists. The latter had kidnapped the governor of North Carolina, and the former were attempting to free him. "Few people know about it," surmised Young, "because the Americans lost the battle and failed

their mission." The mill still exists today and produces a popular flour. If you visit, you will get two for one: a slice of history and a slice of bread.

HAYM SALOMON GRAVESITE · *Mikveh Cemetery, Philadelphia, Pennsylvania*

Mikveh Israel Cemetery, dating from 1740, is one of the oldest Jewish burial grounds in America. A number of distinguished Patriots are buried here, among them Haym Salomon. A businessman from Poland, he helped convert French loans into ready cash by selling bills of exchange for Robert Morris, America's superintendent of finance. In doing so, he helped fund the Revolutionary War. Others buried here are Phillip Moses Russell, a surgeon's mate to General Washington at Valley Forge; and Michael Gratz, who in 1765 signed Maryland's Resolution of Non-Importation, to protest the Stamp Act.

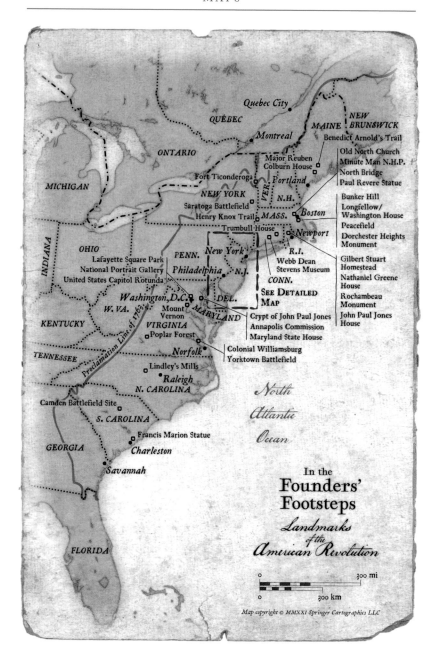

Quebec City
QUÉBEC
Montreal
MAINE
NEW
BRUNSWICK
Benedict Arnold's Trail
ONTARIO
Major Reuben
Colburn House
Old North Church
Minute Man N.H.P.
Fort Ticonderoga
Portland
North Bridge
Paul Revere Statue
MICHIGAN
NEW YORK
VER.
N.H.
Bunker Hill
Longfellow/
Washington House
Saratoga Battlefield
Henry Knox Trail
MASS.
Boston
Peacefield
Trumbull House
Dorchester Heights
Monument
Newport
OHIO
INDIANA
PENN.
New York
R.I.
Gilbert Stuart
Homestead
Lafayette Square Park
National Portrait Gallery
United States Capitol Rotunda
Philadelphia
N.J.
Webb Dean
Stevens Museum
Nathaniel Greene
House
CONN.
Washington,D.C.
DEL.
SEE DETAILED
MAP
Rochambeau
Monument
W. VA.
Mount
Vernon
MARYLAND
Crypt of John Paul Jones
John Paul Jones
House
KENTUCKY
VIRGINIA
Poplar Forest
Annapolis Commission
Maryland State House
TENNESSEE
Norfolk
Colonial Williamsburg
Yorktown Battlefield
Lindley's Mills
Raleigh
N. CAROLINA
Camden Battlefield Site
S. CAROLINA
Francis Marion Statue
GEORGIA
Charleston
Savannah

North
Atlantic
Ocean

In the
Founders'
Footsteps
Landmarks
of the
American Revolution

0   300 mi
0   300 km

Map copyright © MMXXI Springer Cartographics LLC

FLORIDA

Proclamation Line of 1763

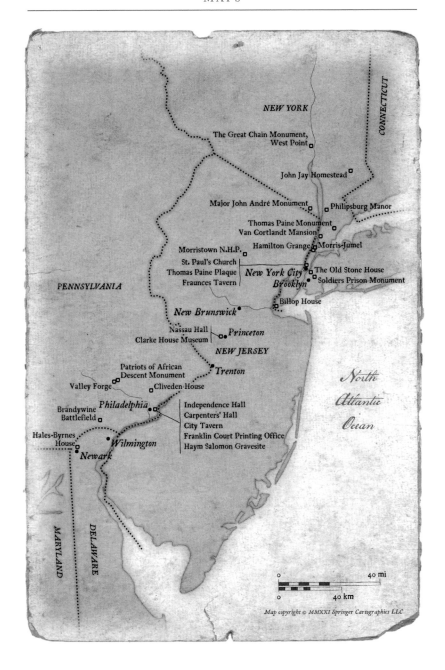

Lafayette was heralded as a Founding Father.

Timeline

꘏

1754   MAY 28: The French and Indian War begins.

1763   FEBRUARY 10: The Treaty of Paris ends the French and Indian War; the English drive the French from North America; the English national debt soars.

       OCTOBER 7: In the Proclamation of 1763, King George III bans colonists from settling beyond the Appalachians.

1764   APRIL 5: The Sugar Act makes it legal for smugglers to be tried in Admiralty Courts without benefit of jury.

1765   MARCH 22: The Stamp Act, which calls for a tax on paper goods and legal documents, is enacted.

       MARCH 24: The Quartering Act holds that colonies must provide housing and food for British troops.

1766   MARCH 18: Parliament repeals the Stamp Act and passes the Declaratory Act, which reinforces Parliament's command over the colonies.

1768   FEBRUARY 11: Massachusetts Assembly issues Massachusetts Circular Letter, denouncing the Townshend Acts, a British measure that taxed goods imported to the American colonies.

       AUGUST 1: The Boston Non-Importation Agreement is signed and Boston merchants agree not to import British goods or export any of their own to England.

1770   MARCH 5: The Boston Massacre takes place.

1772   JUNE 9: Gaspee Affair; a British ship patrolling for smugglers runs aground in Rhode Island and a local mob burns it; members of the mob are accused of treason.

1773   MAY 10: Tea Act is enacted in an attempt by Parliament to undercut smugglers by reducing the price of tea to the colonies.

       DECEMBER 16: Boston Tea Party, during which a cargo of tea was thrown into Boston Harbor, enrages the British.

1774   MARCH 31: Boston Port Act is enacted by Parliament in response to the Tea Party and the port is closed.

SEPTEMBER 5–OCTOBER 26: The First Continental Congress convenes in Carpenters' Hall, Philadelphia.

1775   MARCH 23: Patrick Henry delivers his "Give me liberty or give me death" speech, in Richmond, Virginia.

APRIL 18: Paul Revere and William Dawes ride at midnight to warn Patriots of an imminent British attack.

APRIL 19: Battles of Lexington and Concord (Massachusetts) take place.

MAY 10: Vermont's Ethan Allen and his Green Mountain Boys seize Fort Ticonderoga; the Second Continental Congress meets.

JUNE 15: George Washington is appointed commander in chief.

JUNE 17: Battle of Bunker Hill (Boston) takes place.

JULY 5: Congress approves the Olive Branch Petition, a final attempt to avoid war with England.

NOVEMBER 13: The Americans take Montreal.

DECEMBER 30–JANUARY 1: The Battle of Quebec is fought.

1776   JANUARY 10: Thomas Paine publishes *Common Sense*.

MARCH 1: The British evacuate from Boston.

APRIL 12: Halifax Resolves; North Carolina is the first colony to authorize its delegates to vote for independence.

JUNE 7: Lee Resolution; Richard Henry Lee proposes independence to the Second Continental Congress.

JULY 4: Congress adopts the Declaration of Independence.

AUGUST 27: Battle of Brooklyn (New York) takes place.

SEPTEMBER 15: The British occupy Manhattan.

SEPTEMBER 16: Battle of Harlem Heights (New York) is waged.

SEPTEMBER 22: The British execute soldier spy Nathan Hale, a soldier in the Continental Army.

OCTOBER 28: The Battle of White Plains (New York) is fought.

NOVEMBER 16: Battle of Fort Washington (New York) takes place.

NOVEMBER 20: The British capture Fort Lee (New Jersey).

DECEMBER 23: Thomas Paine publishes *The American Crisis*.

DECEMBER 26: The Battle of Trenton (New Jersey) takes place.

1777 JANUARY 3: The Battle of Princeton (New Jersey) is fought.

JANUARY 6–MAY 28: The Continental Army camps at Morristown, New Jersey.

JUNE 14: Flag Resolution; Congress declares that "the flag of the thirteen United States be thirteen stripes, alternate red and white; that the union be thirteen stars, white in a blue field."

JULY 5: The British capture Fort Ticonderoga.

SEPTEMBER 11: Battle of Brandywine (Pennsylvania) takes place.

SEPTEMBER 20–21: Battle of Paoli (Pennsylvania) is fought.

SEPTEMBER 26: The British take Philadelphia.

OCTOBER 4: The Battle of Germantown (Pennsylvania) is waged.

OCTOBER 7: The Battle of Saratoga (Bemis Heights, New York) begins.

OCTOBER 17: The British surrender at Saratoga.

DECEMBER 19: Washington and his troops set up winter camp in Valley Forge.

1778 FEBRUARY 6: The Americans and France become allies.

FEBRUARY 7: The British general William Howe is replaced by Henry Clinton.

JUNE 18: The British abandon Philadelphia; the Continental Army marches out of Valley Forge.

JUNE 28: The Battle of Monmouth (New Jersey) takes place.

JULY 4: George Rogers Clark captures Kaskaskia, in what is now Illinois.

JULY 29–AUGUST 31: French and American forces besiege Newport, Rhode Island.

DECEMBER 29: The British capture Savannah, Georgia.

1779   JUNE 21: Spain declares war on England.

JULY 16: The Americans capture Stony Point, New York.

SEPTEMBER 16–OCTOBER 19: The American/French attempt to retake Savannah fails.

SEPTEMBER 23: John Paul Jones and the USS *Bonhomme Richard* capture the HMS *Serapis* near the English coast.

NOVEMBER 12: Washington's Main Army begins camping at Morristown, New Jersey.

1780   MAY 12: The British capture Charleston.

MAY 25: The Continental troops of the Pennsylvania line mutiny at Morristown.

MAY 29: The Battle of Waxhaws (South Carolina) is fought.

JULY 11: French troops arrive in Newport, Rhode Island.

AUGUST 16: The Battle of Camden (South Carolina) is waged.

SEPTEMBER 23: The British officer John André is arrested as a spy.

OCTOBER 7: The Battle of Kings Mountain (South Carolina) takes place.

1781   JANUARY 17: The Battle of Cowpens (South Carolina) takes place.

MARCH 2: The Articles of Confederation are adopted; Battle of Clapp's Mill (North Carolina) takes place.

MARCH 15: The Battle of Guilford Courthouse (North Carolina) is fought.

MAY 22–JUNE 18: Siege of Ninety Six (South Carolina) takes place.

SEPTEMBER 8: The Battle of Eutaw Springs (South Carolina) is fought.

SEPTEMBER 13: Battle of Lindley's Mill (North Carolina) takes place.

SEPTEMBER 28–OCTOBER 19: Siege of Yorktown (Virginia) takes place.

OCTOBER 19: General Cornwallis officially surrenders at Yorktown.

1782 MAY 8: American and Spanish forces capture Nassau, Bahamas.

JULY 11: The British leave Savannah.

DECEMBER 14: British evacuate from Charleston.

1783 SEPTEMBER 3: America and England sign the Treaty of Paris.

NOVEMBER 25: The British leave New York City.

DECEMBER 4: Washington bids farewell to his officers in New York City.

DECEMBER 23: Washington resigns as commander in Annapolis.

The delegates convened in this chamber on July 4, 1776.

Who's Who

JOHN ADAMS (1735–1826) was the second president of the United States. His ideas were instrumental in the drafting of the Declaration of Independence.

ABIGAIL ADAMS (1744–1818) was married to John Adams. She had a remarkable mind and her letters to her husband give us important insight to life during the period.

SAMUEL ADAMS (1722–1803), a second cousin of John Adams, was an early leader of the Revolutionary movement.

JOHN ANDRÉ (1751–1780) abetted Benedict Arnold in his attempt to surrender the fort at West Point and was hanged as a British spy.

BENEDICT ARNOLD (1741–1801) fought with distinction for the Continental Army before defecting to the British side, in 1780.

CRISPUS ATTICUS (c. 1723–1770), who was of African and Native American descent, is generally regarded as the first person killed during the Boston Massacre.

JOHN BURGOYNE (1722–1792) was a British army officer who suffered a major defeat at Saratoga.

EDMUND BURKE (1729–1797) while a member of Parliament criticized the British government's treatment of the colonies.

AARON BURR (1756–1836), vice president under President Jefferson, may be better known for killing Alexander Hamilton in a duel in 1804.

BENJAMIN CHEW (1722–1810) was a prominent lawyer whose house was used as a British garrison during the Battle of Germantown.

SIR HENRY CLINTON (1730–1795) served as the British commander in chief in North America in the early stages of the war.

POLLY COOPER (1750-1792), an Oneida woman, aided the soldiers at Valley Forge, traveling hundreds of miles to carry food to the starving men.

CHARLES CORNWALLIS (1738–1805) was the British general whose surrender at Yorktown effectively ended the Revolution.

LYDIA DARRAGH (1721–1789) is thought to have been a secret agent who supplied intelligence to George Washington in British-occupied Philadelphia.

SILAS DEANE (1738–1789) was a delegate to the Continental Congress and later a diplomat assigned to France.

FRANÇOIS DE GRASSE (1722–1788) was a French admiral whose fleet played a crucial role in the rebels' victory at Yorktown.

JOHANN DE KALB (1721–1780), a major general in the Continental Army, was mortally wounded at the Battle of Camden.

JEAN BAPTISTE D'ESTAING (1729–1794), a French admiral, was unsuccessful in forcing the British out of Newport, Rhode Island.

JOHN MURRAY, "LORD DUNMORE" (1730–1809), the colonial governor of Virginia, is noted for "Dunmore's Proclamation," which offered freedom to any slave who fought for the Crown.

BENJAMIN FRANKLIN (1706–1790) was a polymath—author, printer, philosopher, postmaster, scientist, inventor, humorist, and diplomat—who played a pivotal role in persuading the French to join the Americans as an ally.

THOMAS GAGE (1718–1787) was British commander in chief in the early days of the American Revolution.

HORATIO GATES (1727–1806), a rebel general, won acclaim at

the Battle of Saratoga but was condemned for his defeat at Camden.

GEORGE III (1738–1820) was the king of Great Britain for sixty years. He steadfastly opposed American independence.

JOHN GLOVER (1732–1797), a brigadier general in the Continental Army, helped lead the evacuation of Long Island during the Battle of Brooklyn.

NATHANAEL GREENE (1742–1786) was a major general in the Continental Army and Washington's most dependable officer in the southern theater.

NATHAN HALE (1755–1776) was an American spy who was captured by the British and hanged in New York City.

MARY LUDWIG HAYS, "MOLLY PITCHER" (1751–1800), was a legendary figure. She supposedly took her husband's place on the Monmouth battlefield after he fell.

ALEXANDER HAMILTON (1757–1804) was the first secretary of the treasury and a co-author of The Federalist Papers, but is perhaps best remembered for his duel with Aaron Burr.

JOHN HANCOCK (1737–1793) served as president of the Second Continental Congress and is known for his stylish signature on the Declaration of Independence.

PATRICK HENRY (1736–1799) was an American politician and orator. At the Virginia Convention of 1775, he said, "Give me liberty or give me death!"

WILLIAM HOWE (1729–1814) was commander in chief of the British army. He led several campaigns in Canada, among other engagements.

JOHN JAY (1745–1829) was second governor of New York and the first Chief Justice of the United States, as well as a founder of the Federalist Party.

THOMAS JEFFERSON (1743–1826) was the primary author of the Declaration of Independence, a distinguished philosopher and architect, and the third president of the United States.

JOHN PAUL JONES (1747–1792), "Father of the American Navy," had a tempestuous career marked by heroic sea battles and accusations of piracy.

ONA JUDGE (1773–1848) was a slave of Washington's who escaped to freedom in New Hampshire.

HENRY KNOX (1750–1806), an officer of the Continental Army, is remembered for transporting cannons from Fort Ticonderoga to be deployed in the Siege of Boston.

LUCY FLUCKER KNOX (1756–1824), the wife of General Henry Knox, was known for her kindness to soldiers and for severing ties with her Loyalist family.

MARQUIS DE LAFAYETTE (1757–1834) was a French aristocrat who commanded troops at Yorktown. He was a staunch believer in the American cause.

RICHARD HENRY LEE (1732–1794) was an American statesman whose "Lee Resolution" called for the colonies' independence from Great Britain.

BENJAMIN LINCOLN (1733–1810), a major general in the Continental Army, formally accepted the British surrender at Yorktown.

SYBIL LUDINGTON (1761-1839) was considered the "Female Paul Revere" because her legendary forty-mile ride warned the militia that British troops were burning Danbury, Connecticut.

THOMAS MACHIN (1744–1816) was the engineer dispatched by George Washington to design the Great Chain across the Hudson.

JAMES MADISON (1751–1836), the fourth president of the United States, is hailed as the "Father of the Constitution" for his pivotal role in drafting that document and the Bill of Rights.

FRANCIS MARION (1732–1795) was known as the "Swamp Fox" for using guerrilla tactics to aid the Continental Army during the British campaign in South Carolina.

HUGH MERCER (1726–1777), a brigadier general in the Continental Army, died as a result of wounds incurred at the Battle of Princeton.

THOMAS MIFFLIN (1744–1800) was a major general in the Continental army, but was involved in scandals that led to a falling out with Washington.

JAMES MONROE (1758—1831) was the fifth president of the United States. His Monroe Doctrine opposed European colonialism in the Americas.

RICHARD MONTGOMERY (1738–1775), a major general in the Continental Army, died in action during the 1775 invasion of Quebec.

SIR THOMAS MUSGRAVE (1737–1812) was a general in the British Army, noted for his service during the Battle of Germantown.

THOMAS PAINE (1737–1809) was the author of *Common Sense* and *The American Crisis*, the two most influential pamphlets of the Revolution.

FREDERICK PHILIPSE III (1720–1785), a Loyalist, owned a fifty-thousand-acre estate in Westchester County, New York. His house was used by the rebels.

WILLIAM PRESCOTT (1726–1795) commanded the Patriot forces at Bunker Hill. He gave the famous order: "Don't fire until you see the whites of their eyes!"

ISRAEL PUTNAM (1718–1790) was an American general who fought with distinction at Bunker Hill.

PAUL REVERE (1734–1818), silversmith and engraver, is best known for his midnight ride to alert the colonial militia that the British were planning to attack at Lexington and Concord.

JEAN-BAPTISTE DONATIEN DE VIMEUR, COMTE DE RO-
CHAMBEAU (1725–1807) was a French general whose army
played the decisive role in aid of the Americans against the
British at Yorktown.

BENJAMIN RUSH (1745–1813), surgeon general of the Continental Army, was a signer of the Declaration of Independence.

EDWARD RUTLEDGE (1749–1800) was the youngest signatory
of the Declaration. He later became governor of South Carolina.

PETER SALEM (1750-1816), once a slave, participated as a "minute man" at Lexington. He was memorialized in John Trumbull's painting *The Battle of Bunker's Hill*.

HAYM SALOMON (1740–1785) was a Jewish financier who came
to New York City from Poland and helped fund the Continental Army.

MARGARET "PEGGY" SHIPPEN (1760–1804) was married to
Benedict Arnold and is thought to have been a co-conspira-
tor with her husband to surrender at West Point.

LORD STIRLING (1726–1783) was a Scottish-American major
general who distinguished himself at the Battle of Brooklyn.

GILBERT STUART (1755–1828) is widely considered America's
foremost portraitist of George Washington.

BANASTRE TARLETON (1754–1833), a British officer, was
known as the "Butcher" for his ruthless attacks on the rebels.

THAYENDANAGEA, "JOSEPH BRANT" (1743-1807), was an Iroquois leader who during the Revolution convinced other
Iroquois nations to join him in an alliance with the British.

JOHN TRUMBULL (1756–1843) was an American artist (and soldier) who was noted for his historical paintings of the Revolutionary War.

BARON VON STEUBEN (1730–1794), an American military officer, taught the essentials of military drills, tactics, and discipline.

GEORGE WASHINGTON (1732–1799), "Father of His Country," was commander in chief of the Continental Army and the first president of the United States.

MARTHA WASHINGTON (1731–1802), was the wife of George Washington. She is known for her devotion to the troops and her frequent visits to them at their winter quarters.

"MAD" ANTHONY WAYNE (1745–1796) was an American officer whose military exploits and fiery personality earned him his nickname.

PHILLIS WHEATLEY (1753–1784) was the first African American author of a published book of poetry and is known, too, for her brief correspondence with George Washington.

Washington was a frequent visitor to St. Paul's Chapel.

ACKNOWLEDGMENTS

❧

I'm extremely grateful to the many people who generously assisted to make this book possible. For editing suggestions and critiques of the manuscript, I'm thankful to Barnet Schecter, Paula Cooper, and Chip McGrath, each of whom contributed invaluably. I'm indebted to those who conducted tours, especially Fred Cookinham, of In-Depth Tours; Mary McLeod and Bill Troppman, of the National Park Service; Will Krakower, of the Clarke House at Princeton; and Carolyn Wallace, of Cliveden Manor. Ann Lucas, of the Thomas Jefferson Foundation, was particularly helpful with her knowledge of Poplar Forest and Monticello.

My good friends Jack Kerr and Bob Demento extended themselves to arrange private visits to the Princeton Battlefield and Independence Hall, respectively. Ed Strauss introduced me to the Revolutionary War Roundtable, a monthly gathering of history buffs, which has been a great resource for my project. Matt Viederman, a classmate from our college days, had many illuminating thoughts on the background of the Revolution and I'm thankful for his suggestion to read Rick Atkinson's two-volume work on this period. Chip Fisher was a companion on various site visits, among them the Conference House on Staten Island.

I'm exceedingly grateful to all those librarians and researchers who offered their time and knowledge to assist my efforts. In particular, Ellen Cohn, of the Franklin Papers at Yale University, provided considerable information. Andrew Berner and Scott Overall, at the University Club library in New York, allowed me to use the reference room to work with the primary sources that are part of the club's collection. Several curators, historians, and journalists imparted their knowledge when I sought their perspective on various sites. Colonel James Johnson, at Marist College, and Officer Sean Scully, at West Point, were instructive about Benedict Arnold's role at Saratoga and about the Great Chain along the Hudson. Professor Jim Martin, at the University of Houston, shared his experience following Arnold's route to Quebec; Ann Burton was helpful regarding the Webb House, where she has worked for several years; and Bernard Drew provided critical details about General Knox's trek through Massachusetts en route to Boston from Fort Ticonderoga.

Evan Thomas was kind enough to meet me in New York to discuss his biography of John Paul Jones. The historian David McCullough has been a frequent adviser, not only as a passionate chronicler of the Revolutionary period, but also as a friend. I've read his book *1776* numerous times, and listened to his narration as well, and learned more and more with each experience. I owe much to my contacts and fellow faculty at Yale, especially Professors John Witt, Paul Kennedy, and Jay Gitlin, who inspired me to delve deeper into the stories behind certain landmarks, such as Germantown and Saratoga.

The publishers and editors at Godine, particularly David Godine himself, Joshua Bodwell, and Sue Ramin, were supportive from the beginning, and I thank them for their enthusiasm and encouragement. The book's designer, Jerry Kelly, is the creative talent behind the layout, and Nick Springer, of Cartographics, made excellent maps to accompany the text. Thank you to Nathaniel Philbrick for writing the preface, and for making time to meet in Nantucket to discuss Washington's military leadership.

I'd like to thank for their input at various stages: Phyllis Dillon, Roger Angell, Gary Shapiro, Camille Valentine, Stephanie Koven, Scott Hirsch, Lindley Young, Anne Close, Ed Sorel,

Steve Wilson, Louisa McCullough, David Schiff, Nora Kerr, Tom Fleming, and Sidney Offit. And thank you to my students at Yale, who often provided inspiration.

My parents, John and Mira Van Doren, always supportive, provided useful critiques of the essays and the artwork.

Special thanks go to my wife, Charlotte, who came up with the concept for this project, and to my children, Abbott and Henry, who were always happy to express their thoughts and who stimulated me with their revelations.

Like Cincinattus, Washington returned to his farm at Mount Vernon.

Select Bibliography

✣

Adams, John Quincy. *Oration on the Life and Character of Gilbert Motier de Lafayette*. Washington, D.C.: Gales and Seaton, 1835.

Ansary, Cyrus A. *George Washington Dealmaker-in-Chief*. Washington, D.C.: Lambert Publications, 2019.

Atkinson, Rick. *The British Are Coming: The War for America, Lexington to Princeton, 1775-1777*. New York: Henry Holt and Co., 2019.

Baker, Mark Allen. *Connecticut Families of the Revolution: American Forebears from Burr to Wolcott*. Charleston, S.C.: The History Press, 2014.

Bales, Richard. *The Columbia Records Legacy Collection: American Revolution*. Washington, D.C.: National Gallery of Art, 1960.

Berkin, Carol. *Revolutionary Mothers: Women in the Struggle for America's Independence*. New York: Alfred A. Knopf, 2005.

Bill, Alfred Hoyt. *Valley Forge: The Making of an Army*. New York: Harper and Brothers, 1952.

Bliven, Bruce, Jr. *Battle for Manhattan*. New York: Henry Holt and Co., 1955.

Boatner, Mark Mayo, III. *Encyclopedia of the American Revolution*. New York: David McKay Company, 1966.

Bradford, Alden. *Biographical Notices of Distinguished Men in New England*. Boston: S. G. Simpkins Publisher, 1842.

Brown, Richard H., and Paul E. Cohen. *Revolution: Mapping the Road to American Independence, 1775-1783*. New York: W. W. Norton, 2015.

Calloway, Colin G. *The Indian World of George Washington*. New York: Oxford University Press, 2018.

Chernow, Ron. *Alexander Hamilton*. New York: Penguin Books, 2005.

Commager, Henry Steele, and Richard B. Morris, eds. *The Spirit of 'Seventy-Six*. New York: Bobbs Merrill Co., 1958.

Dearborn, Henry. *Revolutionary War Journals of Henry Dearborn, 1775–1783*. Edited by Lloyd A. Brown and Howard H. Peckham. New York: The Caxton Club, 1939.

Drew, Bernard A. *Henry Knox and the Revolutionary War Train in Western Massachusetts*. Jefferson, N.C.: McFarland and Co., 2012.

Ferris, Robert G., and James H. Charleton, eds. *Signers of the Declaration*. Washington, D.C.: US Department of the Interior, 1975.

Fischer, David Hackett. *Washington's Crossing*. New York: Oxford University Press, 2004.

Fleming, Thomas. *Beat the Last Drum: The Siege of Yorktown, 1781*. New York: St. Martin's Press, 1963.

Flexner, James Thomas. *Washington: The Indispensable Man*. New York: Back Bay Books, 1994.

Forbes, Esther. *Paul Revere and the World He Lived In*. Boston: Houghton Mifflin, 1942.

Gelb, Norman. *Less Than Glory: A Revisionist's View of the American Revolution*. New York: G. P. Putnam's Sons, 1984.

Gitlin, Jay. *The Bourgeois Frontier: French Towns, French Traders & American Expansion*. New Haven, Conn.: Yale University Press, 2010.

Graves, Robert. "The Case for the Forgotten Loyalist," *The Columbia Records Legacy Collection: American Revolution*. Washington, D.C.: National Gallery of Art, 1960.

Gifford, Edward S., Jr. *The American Revolution in the Delaware Valley*. Philadelphia: Pennsylvania Society of Sons of the Revolution, 1976.

Gigantino, James J., II, ed. *The American Revolution in New Jersey*. New Brunswick, N.J.: Rutgers University Press, 2015.

Gutzman, Kevin R. C. *Thomas Jefferson, Revolutionary: A Radical's Struggle to Remake America*. New York: St. Martin's Press, 2017.

Hagist, Don N. *The Revolution's Last Men: The Soldiers Behind the Photographs*. Yardley, Pa.: Westholme, 2015.

Homans, Abigail Adams. *Education by Uncles*. Boston: Houghton Mifflin, 1966.

Hook, Sidney. Introduction to *The Essential Thomas Paine*, xvii–xix. New York: New American Library, 1969.

Kamensky, Jane. *A Revolution in Color: The World of John Singleton Copley*. New York: W. W. Norton, 2016.

Johnson, Gerald W. *The First Captain: The Story of John Paul Jones*. New York: Coward-McCann, 1947.

Jones, Charles C., ed. *The Siege of Savannah in 1779*. Albany: Joel Munsell Publishers, 1874.

Kennedy, Frances H. *The American Revolution, A Historical Guidebook*. New York: Oxford University Press, 2014.

Ketchum, Richard R., ed. *The American Heritage Book of the Revolution*. New York: American Heritage Publishing Company, 1958.

Kiernan, Denise, and Joseph D'Agnese. *Signing Their Lives Away: The Fame and Misfortune of the Men Who Signed the Declaration of Independence*. Philadelphia: Quirk Books, 2009.

Knoblock, Glenn A. *"Strong and Brave Fellows": New Hampshire's Black Soldiers and Sailors of the American Revolution, 1775–1784*. Jefferson, N.C.: McFarland and Co., 2003.

Konstam, Angus. *Guilford Courthouse, 1781: Lord Cornwallis's Ruinous Victory*. Westport, Conn.: Praeger, 2004.

Lepore, Jill. "The Sharpened Quill," *The New Yorker*, Oct. 16, 2006.

Little, David B. *America's First Centennial Celebration*. Boston: Houghton Mifflin, 1974.

Lossing, Benson John. *A Pictorial Field Book of the American Revolution*. New York: Harper and Brothers, 1859.

McCullough, David. *1776*. New York: Simon & Schuster, 2005.

____. *John Adams*. New York: Simon & Schuster, 2002.

McGuire, Thomas J. *The Surprise of Germantown*. Philadelphia: Cliveden of the National Trust for Historic Preservation and Thomas Publications, 1994.

Miller, Helen Hill. *George Mason, Constitutionalist*. New York: Simon Publications, 1938.

Moody, Sid. *'76: The World Turned Upside Down*. New York: The Associated Press, 1975.

Morgan, Edmund S. *American Heroes*. New York: W. W Norton, 2009.

Moyers, Bill. *Moyers: Report from Philadelphia: The Constitutional Convention of 1787*. New York: Ballantine Books, 1987.

Newlin, Algie I. *The Battle of Lindley's Mill*. Burlington, N.C. The Alamance Historical Association, 1975.

Nichols, Frederick Doveton. *Thomas Jefferson's Architectural Drawings*. Charlottesville, Va.: Thomas Jefferson Memorial Foundation, 1961.

Oller, John. *The Swamp Fox: How Francis Marion Saved the American Revolution*. Boston: Da Capo Press, 2016.

Paine, Thomas. *Common Sense*. Reprint, Dublin, Ohio: Coventry House Publications, 2016.

Philbrick, Nathaniel. *In the Hurricane's Eye: The Genius of George Washington and the Victory at Yorktown*. New York: Viking Press, 2018.

Quarles, Benjamin. *The Negro in the American Revolution*. Chapel Hill: University of North Carolina Press, 1961.

Raphael, Ray. *Founding Myths: Stories That Hide Our Patriotic Past*. New York: MJF Books, 2004.

Raymond, Henry J. *An Oration Pronounced Before the Young Men of Westchester County on the Completion of the Monument Erected by Them to the Captors of Major André*. New Haven, Conn.: Yale University Press, 2010.

Rhodehamel, John, ed. *The American Revolution. Writings from the War of Independence*. New York: Library of America, 2001.

Roberts, Kenneth. *Cowpens: The Great Morale-Builder*. Portland, Maine: Westholme Publications, 1957.

Ronald, D. A. B. *The Life of Major André: The Redcoat Who Turned Benedict Arnold*. Philadelphia: Casemate, 2019.

Rush, Benjamin. *Letters of Benjamin Rush*. Edited by Lyman H. Butterfield. 2 vols. Princeton, N.J.: Princeton University Press, 1951.

Schecter, Barnet. *The Battle for New York*. New York: Walker Books, 2002.

___. *George Washington's America: A Biography Through His Maps*. New York: Walker Books, 2010.

Sloane, Eric, and Eric Hatch. *A Celebration of Bells*. Mineola, N.Y.: Dover Publications, 1964.

Stember, Sol. *The Bicentennial Guide to the American Revolution, Vol. III: The War in the South*. New York: E. P. Dutton, 1974.

Thomas, Evan. *John Paul Jones: Sailor, Hero, Father of the American Navy*. New York: Simon & Schuster, 2003.

Trevelyan, George Otto. *The American Revolution*. New York: David McKay and Co., 1899.

Tuchman, Barbara W. *The First Salute: A View of the American Revolution*. New York: Ballantine Books, 1989.

Van Doren, Carl. *Benjamin Franklin*. New York: Viking Press, 1938.

___. *Secret History of the American Revolution.* New York: Viking Press, 1941.

Ward, Carol S. *Morris-Jumel Mansion.* Charleston, S.C.: Arcadia Publishing, 2015.

Ware, Susan, ed. *Forgotten Heroes.* New York: Free Press, 1998.

Washington, George. *Orderly Book of General George Washington, Kept at Valley Forge May 18–June 10, 1778.* New York: Lamson Wolff and Co., 1898.

Wood, Gordon S. *The American Revolution: A History.* New York: Modern Library, 2003.

Woodhull, Alfred A. *The Battle of Princeton: A Preliminary Study.* Princeton, N.J.: W. C. Sinclair, 1913.

Wright, Esmond, ed. *The Fire of Liberty.* New York: St. Martin's Press, 1983.

Wulf, Andrea. *Founding Gardeners.* New York: Alfred A. Knopf, 2011.

Yorktown Sesquicentennial Association (various authors). *The Yorktown Book: The Official Tribute and Chronicle Book.* Richmond, Va.: Whittet and Shepperson, 1932.

Young, Alfred F. *Masquerade: The Life and Times of Deborah Sampson, Continental Soldier.* New York: Alfred A. Knopf, 2004.

Set in Caslon types.
Book design by
Jerry Kelly.